ACHIEVING GREATER ECONOMIC DEVELOPMENT IN KAZAKHSTAN THROUGH FISCAL DECENTRALIZATION AND EQUALIZATION

DECEMBER 2025

ASIAN DEVELOPMENT BANK

ADB

6 ADB Avenue, Mandaluyong City, 1550 Metro Manila, Philippines
Tel +63 2 8632 4444; Fax +63 2 8636 2444
www.adb.org

ISBN 978-92-9277-606-0 (print); 978-92-9277-607-7 (PDF); 978-92-9277-608-4 (ebook)
Publication Stock No. TCS250526-2
DOI: http://dx.doi.org/10.22617/TCS250526-2

Notes:
In this publication, "$" refers to United States dollars and "T" refers to tenge.
ADB recognizes "China" as the People's Republic of China and "Korea" as the Republic of Korea.
The boundaries, colors, denominations, and any other information shown on the maps do not imply, on the part of the Asian Development Bank, any judgment on the legal status of any territory, or any other endorsement or acceptance of such boundaries, colors, denominations, or information.

Cover design by Josef Ilumin.

CONTENTS

TABLES, FIGURES, AND BOXES

TABLES

FIGURES

BOXES

ACKNOWLEDGMENTS

Achieving Greater Economic Development in Kazakhstan Through Fiscal Decentralization and Equalization was prepared under the auspices of the Joint Government of Kazakhstan and Asian Development Bank (ADB) Knowledge and Experience Exchange Program, Phase 5 (TA 10150-KAZ).

The study was carried out under the overall supervision of Utsav Kumar, ADB country director for Kazakhstan, and Asel Sarsenbayeva, chair of the board of JSC Economic Research Institute (ERI). Andrés Rodríguez-Pose, Princesa de Asturias chair and professor of economic geography at the London School of Economics and Political Science, led the study with the support and co-authorship of Federico Bartalucci, economic development consultant, and the team of ERI under the Ministry of National Economy of the Republic of Kazakhstan (MNE): Kaisar Nigmetov, deputy chair of the Management Board of ERI; Ksenia Zagal, director of the Center for Fiscal Policy of ERI; Elmira Ossipova, deputy director of the Center for Fiscal Policy of ERI; and Meruyert Zhumakhan, senior expert of the Center for Fiscal Policy of ERI.

The study was guided by Yerlan Sagnaev, director of the Department of Tax and Customs Policy of MNE; Saltanat Omarova, head of the Division of Analysis and Forecasting of Tax and Non-Tax Revenues of the Department of Tax and Customs Policy of MNE; Bibinur Kurmasheva, director of the Department of Tax and Customs Legislation of the Ministry of Finance of the Republic of Kazakhstan (MOF); and Olzhas Beisembayev, director of the Budget Legislation Department of MOF.

Roy Bahl, as peer reviewer, contributed invaluable insights and constructive comments, enriching the quality and rigor of the study. Also, the study greatly benefited from the support and suggestions of Sandeep Bhattacharya, principal public sector specialist, from ADB's Asia Pacific Tax Hub.

Genadiy Rau, senior economics officer, ADB Kazakhstan Resident Mission; and Saltanat Yunussova and Arman Mussin, ADB consultants, participated in the design of the research and provided support throughout the study, including guidance during the data sourcing and the drafting process.

The study was initiated at the request of the Department of Budget Policy of MNE.

We express gratitude to Rodel S. Bautista who coordinated the editorial and publication process with the following ADB consultants: Margaret Ruth Griffiths (copyediting), Maria Guia de Guzman (proofreading), Ma. Cecilia Abellar (proof checking), Alvin Tubio (typesetting), and Josef Ilumin (cover design).

ABBREVIATIONS

ADB	Asian Development Bank
BRT	Bus Rapid Transit
PRC	People's Republic of China
CGC	Commonwealth Grants Commission
CIT	corporate income tax
DTI	Development Trap Index
EAEU	Eurasian Economic Union
ERI	Economic Research Institute
FPE	State Participation Fund
FPM	Municipal Participation Fund
GDP	gross domestic product
GRP	gross regional product
ICMS	Tax on Circulation of Goods and Services
MOF	Ministry of Finance
OECD	Organisation for Economic Co-operation and Development
PIT	personal income tax
PPP	public–private partnership
R&D	research and development
RTS	Representative Tax System
RWI	Regional Wellbeing Index
SALGA	South African Local Government Association
SDPP	state district power plant
SEZ	special economic zone
SMEs	small and medium-sized enterprises
VAT	value-added tax

EXECUTIVE SUMMARY

Kazakhstan has ambitious growth plans, including reaching high-income status and implementing a comprehensive economic development strategy until 2029. Its rate of economic growth since the 1990s has been impressive, unlike many countries that are struggling to make the transition from low- to middle-income status. However, this growth has been highly volatile: it has relied heavily on commodity prices, which has rendered the country's growth path vulnerable to commodity shocks. Moreover, the growth rate has somewhat slowed in the past 5 years relative to other middle-income countries. There are also growing concerns that Kazakhstan may be entering a "middle-income trap"—that is, a period of stagnation stemming from an inability to transition the economy from natural resource dependency toward other, knowledge-intensive, economic sectors and activities. To boost economic growth, Kazakhstan recently launched its National Development Plan until 2029, focusing on developing five key pillars: stimulating competitiveness, developing entrepreneurship, fostering human capital development, boosting innovation and digitalization, and reducing regional inequalities.

Innovation-driven competitiveness and solid economic ecosystems are vital to Kazakhstan's efforts to diversify its economy and enhance dynamism across all its constituent regions and, consequently, the whole country. The rapid economic growth witnessed over the past 3 decades has been concentrated mainly in resource-rich areas and urban centers. Indices of competitiveness and innovation reveal significant imbalances across the country, with the southern and eastern regions displaying lower economic dynamism and higher risks of medium- and long-term stagnation. These territorial inequalities threaten to undermine Kazakhstan's growth ambitions. To address this, the development of innovation ecosystems—centered around high-quality infrastructure, support for local firms, a highly skilled workforce, and robust inward investment—is essential for revitalizing lagging local economies.

To realize this vision, Kazakhstan must harness its full economic potential. This requires sound development strategies identifying latent potential, wherever it can be found in the country, as well as resources to implement these strategies.

Fiscal decentralization offers the means to mobilize this potential. If used appropriately, it can become a powerful mechanism for economic growth. The concept of fiscal decentralization has increasingly been recognized as a tool to enhance fiscal capacity and local tax revenues and to allow local governments to implement development strategies. Examples from Brazil, the People's Republic of China, and Germany highlight the potential of fiscal decentralization as an engine for growth. Granting local fiscal autonomy can foster policy experimentation, improve efficiency, and enhance accountability. However, Kazakhstan must address several bottlenecks to enable successful tax devolution.

Kazakhstan needs to choose carefully what type of fiscal decentralization to implement. Various decentralization scenarios exist for the country, from providing subnational governments with greater flexibility in using revenues to enabling the local retention of national tax revenues. However, as a traditionally centralized state, Kazakhstan needs to consider substantial reforms to ensure subnational institutions have the capacity to manage these additional resources efficiently.

With increased decentralization, an effective redistribution and equalization system will be critical to address territorial disparities. Fiscal decentralization and equalization are closely linked: stronger tax devolution at the local level requires robust equalization systems to mitigate imbalances in fiscal residuals and expenditure capacity. Best practices from Australia, Canada, and Germany suggest the need for independent oversight of equalizing funds, a flexible yet predictable system, and regularly updated distribution formulas. For Kazakhstan, incorporating new variables, such as regional wellbeing, could significantly enhance equity while aligning with the Organisation for Economic Co-operation and Development's best practices. This report explores 10 potential scenarios incorporating diverse demographic, geographical, and socioeconomic factors.

A wide range of policy recommendations for both central and subnational governments emerge from international case studies. Greater fiscal decentralization and stronger fiscal redistribution across Kazakhstan's oblasts require action across all tiers of government. The central government needs to consider establishing capacity-building programs for administrators, ensuring greater data transparency, and providing a clearer framework for fiscal responsibilities across different tiers of government. It should also provide the framework to improve multilevel governance while simultaneously designing an equitable formula-based equalization system, ideally managed by an independent body that regularly monitors the fiscal redistribution criteria. Concurrently, subnational governments will need to put in place sufficient financial management capacity, prioritize critical service areas, and establish robust monitoring systems. Promoting regional collaboration across oblasts will facilitate the sharing of best practices.

Ultimately, an integrated approach to devolving fiscal autonomy will, first, ensure no region in Kazakhstan is left behind, while simultaneously leading to greater overall economic growth and development in the country. This ultimately means establishing a new growth paradigm for Kazakhstan, one that delivers a more equitable, prosperous, and dynamic economy across territories in the country.

INTRODUCTION

1

Since Kazakhstan gained independence in December 1991, its economy has undergone profound transformations. In the aftermath of the Soviet Union's dissolution, the country embarked on building national institutions and transitioning from a centrally planned economy to a market-driven system. Figure 1 shows the evolution of gross domestic product (GDP) growth rates across Kazakhstan, Europe and Central Asia, and middle-income countries from 1991 to 2023.

Kazakhstan experienced significant economic upheavals during the 1990s, with GDP contracting by approximately 36% between 1990 and 1995 as a result of the collapse of its heavy industry. Although the economy began recovering between 1995 and 1997, the Russian financial crisis in 1998, coupled with declining oil prices, caused GDP to decline by roughly 2% in 1998 (World Bank 2024a). Despite these initial setbacks, Kazakhstan recorded robust economic growth during much of the period between 2000 and 2014. Oil rents exceeded 10% of GDP during this time, averaging 15% between 2005 and 2014 and peaking at 21% in 2005 (World Bank 2024a). In 2006, Kazakhstan entered the upper middle-income group of countries; until 2013, its economic growth frequently outpaced that of other Central Asian and middle-income nations (Figure 1).

Figure 1: Gross Domestic Product Growth Rate Across Kazakhstan, Eastern Europe and Central Asia (excluding high-income), and Middle-Income Countries, 1991–2023

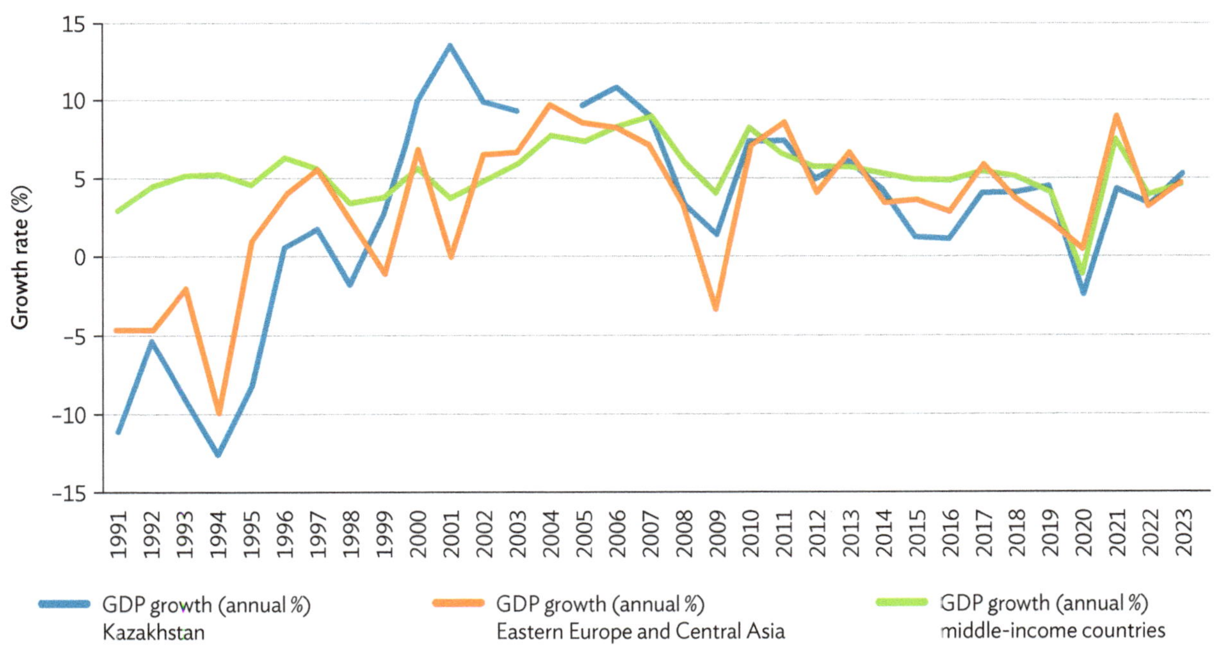

GDP = gross domestic product.

Note: The aggregate measure for Eastern Europe and Central Asia excludes high-income countries in the region.

Source: Authors' elaboration based on World Bank (2024a).

Figures 2 and 3 highlight annual GDP growth per capita and GDP per capita for Kazakhstan, Eastern Europe and Central Asia (excluding high-income countries), and other middle-income nations from 1991 to 2023. Kazakhstan's GDP per capita fell sharply in the early 1990s following independence, reflecting the economic contraction caused by its transition to a market-driven economy. By the mid-1990s, GDP per capita had declined to below $1,500 (current $). Recovery commenced in the late 1990s, with growth accelerating in the early 2000s, driven by economic reforms, oil revenues, and increased investment. By 2007, GDP per capita had exceeded $8,000. Following a brief slowdown during the 2008 global financial crisis, growth resumed, peaking above $13,000 in the early 2010s. After a dip in 2015, caused by falling oil prices and the Russian economic crisis, GDP per capita stabilized at approximately $13,100 by 2023.

Figure 2: Gross Domestic Product per Capita Growth Across Kazakhstan, Eastern Europe and Central Asia (excluding high-income), and Middle-Income Countries, 1991–2023

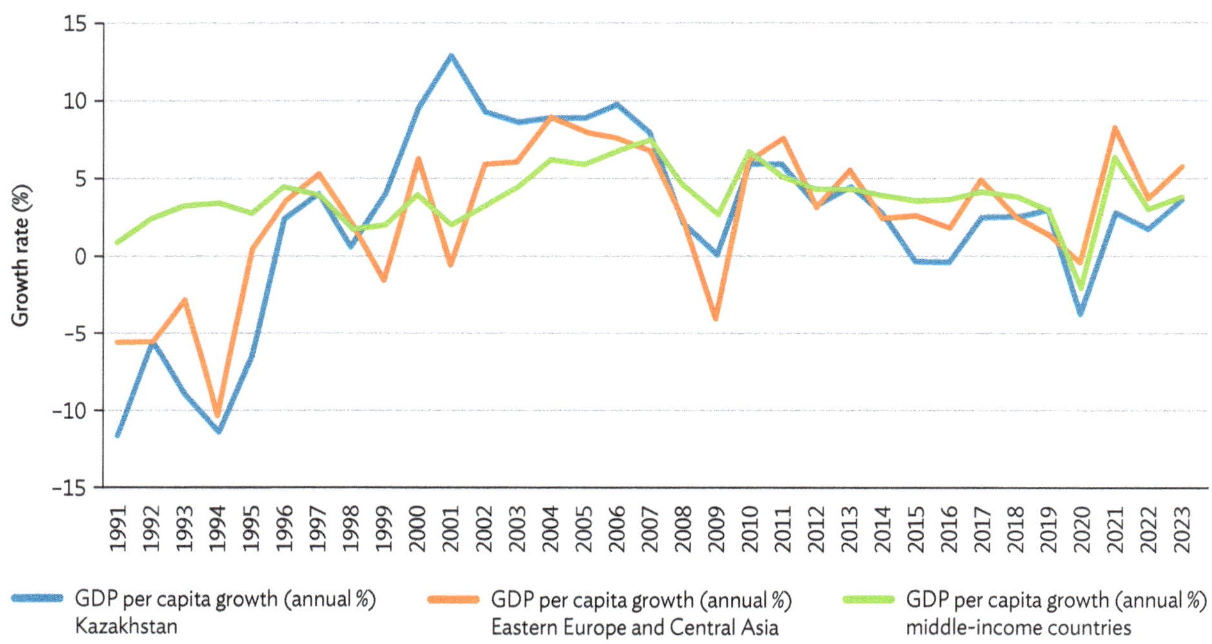

GDP = gross domestic product.

Note: The aggregate measure for Eastern Europe and Central Asia excludes high-income countries in the region.

Source: Authors' elaboration based on World Bank (2024a).

Kazakhstan's economic growth has been marked by greater volatility than that of other Central Asian and middle-income economies. The orange line in Figure 2—representing middle- and low-income countries in Eastern Europe and Central Asia—indicates a more stable trajectory. After a slight decline in the early 1990s, the region followed a relatively steady growth path from the 2000s onward. While the 2008 financial crisis caused temporary stagnation, the region's GDP per capita recovered and continued an upward trend, reaching just under $8,500 by 2023. Middle-income countries exhibited similarly stable growth throughout this period.

Figure 3: Gross Domestic Product per Capita Across Kazakhstan, Eastern Europe and Central Asia (excluding high-income), and Middle-Income Countries, 1991–2023

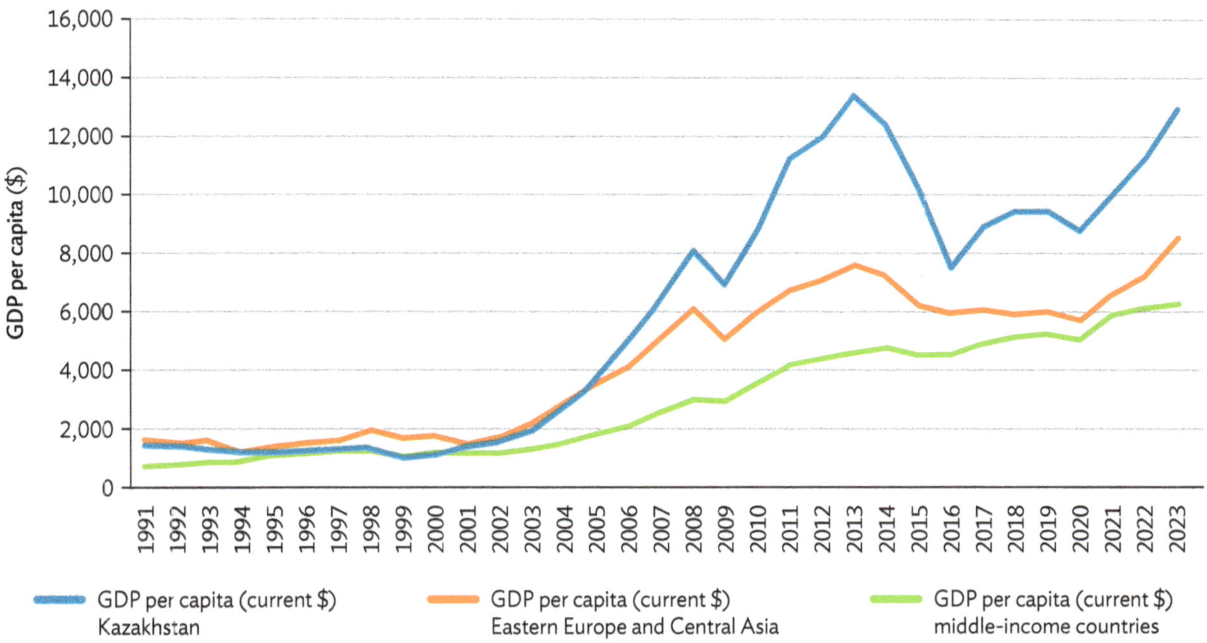

GDP = gross domestic product.

Note: The aggregate measure for Europe and Central Asia excludes high-income countries in the region.

Source: Authors' elaboration based on World Bank (2024a).

Kazakhstan's economy is particularly susceptible to volatility linked to the economy of the Russian Federation—its key trade partner—and to fluctuations in commodity prices, especially oil (ADB 2018). Although Kazakhstan's economic growth outpaced that of other Central Asian countries during the 2000s, it has often lagged behind since the 2007–2008 global financial crisis, particularly following the 2015 commodity crisis. This slowdown is frequently attributed to the country's limited economic diversification (OECD 2024b). Despite reforms since the 1990s aimed at increasing private sector contributions, diversifying employment and output, and integrating into regional and global value chains, the economy remains heavily reliant on hydrocarbons and metals (OECD 2024b). Moreover, declining trend growth over the past 2 decades indicates that the commodity sector's surge has not been matched by corresponding productivity increases in non-resource sectors (ADB 2024).

Diversifying Kazakhstan's export basket remains a high priority for policymakers. Over the past 2 decades, the country has achieved moderate geographic diversification, with export markets now comparable to those of some Organisation for Economic Co-operation and Development (OECD) nations (OECD 2024b). However, sectoral diversification remains limited, with hydrocarbon products constituting over 53% of exports and 15% of GDP in 2023 (IMF 2024). Recent initiatives include promoting small and medium-sized enterprises (SMEs) through export-support policies, improving transport infrastructure, and enhancing trade facilitation in key hubs (OECD 2024b).

Figure 4: Representation of the Regional Wellbeing Index, 2023

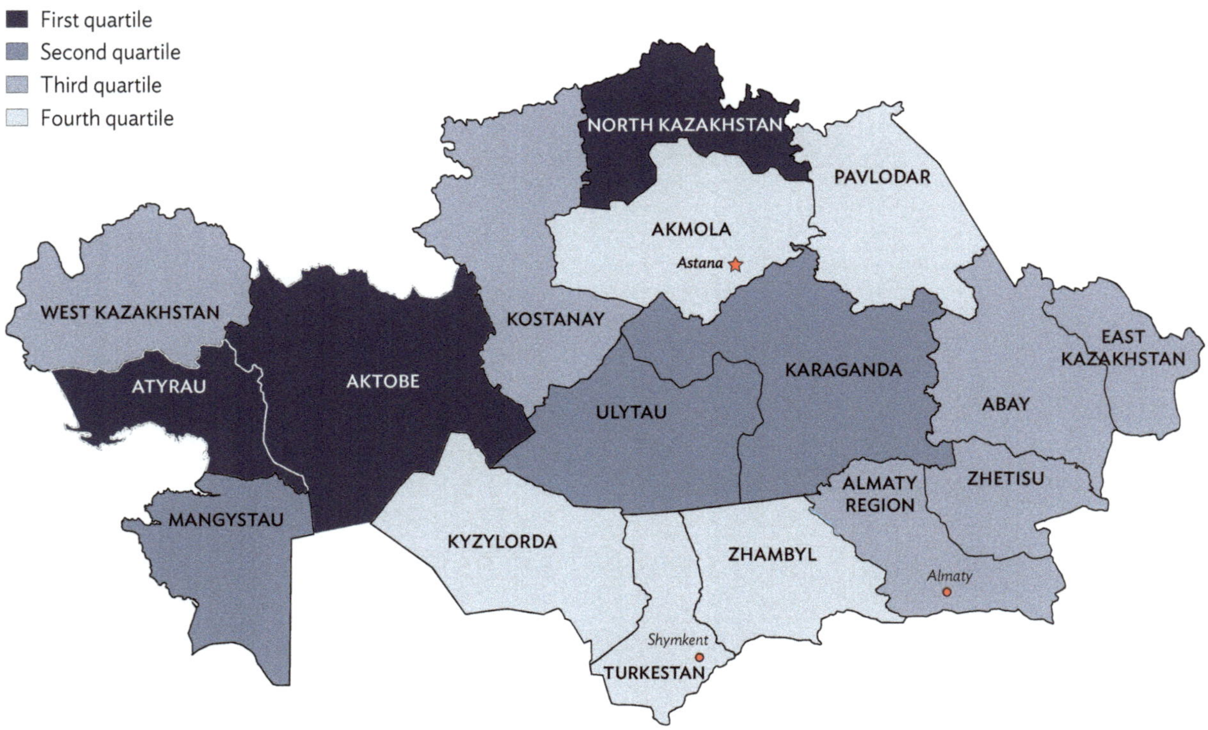

Source: Rodríguez-Pose et al. (2024b).

Economic growth over the past 2 decades has also been accompanied by rising territorial inequalities. Studies reveal significant disparities among oblasts in terms of income, health care, education, and security (Rodríguez-Pose et al. 2024a). Urban areas such as Astana, Almaty city, and Shymkent, alongside resource-rich western oblasts like Atyrau, show higher levels of wellbeing, while southern oblasts, including Zhambyl, Pavlodar, and Turkestan, consistently underperform. Figure 4 maps the Regional Wellbeing Index, encompassing measures of income, work quality, housing, and governance.

Although Kazakhstan's GDP per capita has grown significantly over the past 2 decades, the benefits have been unevenly distributed, accruing mainly to a limited number of regions (Rodríguez-Pose and Bartalucci 2021). Economic gains from growth and global market integration have been far more constrained in other areas. These disparities represent considerable opportunity costs and heighten the risk of social unrest. Lagging regions remain untapped potential for socioeconomic development. Evidence increasingly suggests large territorial inequalities not only present equity issues but also represent barriers to national efficiency and growth (European Commission 2024; Rodríguez-Pose et al. 2024b). Such disparities also risk fostering discontent and anti-establishment sentiments, which could escalate into significant unrest (Rodríguez-Pose 2018).

Progressive taxation and fiscal policies are widely regarded as effective tools for promoting economic growth and reducing territorial inequalities. Fiscal decentralization—the delegation of taxing and spending authority from central to regional or local governments—and fiscal redistribution through progressive taxation and transfers can mobilize untapped potential across the country. These mechanisms have considerable potential to reduce disparities, particularly by enhancing the fiscal capacity of less-developed regions (Chernick 2003; Blöchlinger et al. 2007; Dougherty and Forman 2021). As Kazakhstan prepares for comprehensive tax reform by 2026, these tools become even more relevant, with significant changes expected in tax rates and the allocation of collection responsibilities.

This report examines Kazakhstan's options for fiscal decentralization and equalization, analyzing the challenges and conditions required to devolve greater powers to local authorities. It explores the creation of equitable redistribution systems designed to address socioeconomic disparities across the country's oblasts in pursuit of greater, more balanced, and sustainable economic growth.[1]

1 While this report specifically addresses the revenue dimension of fiscal decentralization, it is important to highlight that fiscal decentralization comprises not only revenue assignment but also expenditure responsibilities. Indeed, the effectiveness of fiscal decentralization in promoting local autonomy and accountability is significantly influenced by the degree of expenditure decentralization, as the capacity of local governments to allocate resources according to local priorities plays a critical role in achieving sustainable and inclusive economic growth. This duality of fiscal decentralization—often summarized by the maxim "finance flows function"—should be comprehensively explored in subsequent analyses. Although this report, given its initial project parameters, does not provide a detailed analysis or calculations related to expenditure decentralization, future research should explicitly integrate this dimension to offer a more holistic assessment of Kazakhstan's fiscal decentralization strategy. Work on the report lasted from August 2024 to February 2025, in parallel with the process of developing the new Budget Code of the Republic of Kazakhstan. In this regard, certain provisions of the report refer to the Budget Code in force before the adoption of the new Budget Code, as well as to the draft of the new Budget Code posted on the website of the Majilis of the Parliament of the Republic of Kazakhstan dated 28 September 2023: https://mazhilis.parlam.kz/#/all-bill/pending-majilis.

KAZAKHSTAN'S ECONOMIC GROWTH AMBITIONS

2

A New Way Forward: Kazakhstan National Development Plan

Kazakhstan has embarked on a series of ambitious reforms to modernize its economy and enhance governance. Central to these reforms is the Kazakhstan National Development Plan, launched in 2024, which outlines the country's long-term vision of doubling nominal GDP by 2029, based on 2023 levels (Sakenova 2024). The strategy focuses on five key areas: (i) stimulating competitiveness, (ii) developing entrepreneurship, (iii) fostering human capital development, (iv) boosting innovation and digitalization, and (v) reducing regional inequalities (Figure 5).

Figure 5: Strategic Priorities for Kazakhstan National Development Plan

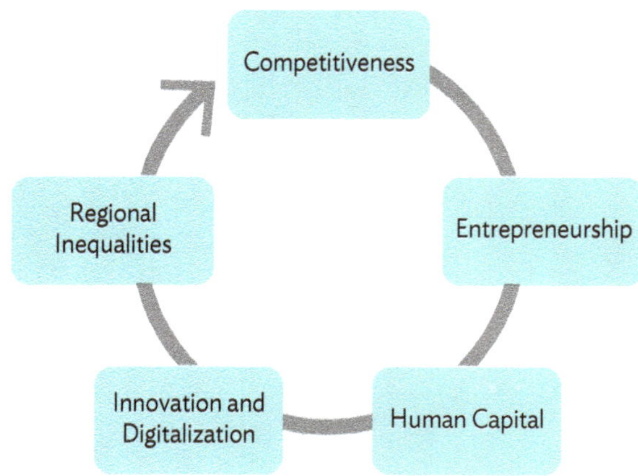

Source: Authors' elaboration based on Sakenova (2024).

To achieve the objectives outlined in the National Development Plan, Kazakhstan has implemented a series of policies designed to accelerate economic transformation. To stimulate competitiveness, the country has pursued economic diversification initiatives aimed at reducing its reliance on natural resources by promoting sectors such as manufacturing, agriculture, and services (OECD 2020b). Efforts have also been made to improve the business environment through public governance reforms, creating a more favorable climate for investments and sustainable growth. However, challenges persist, including an overdependence on natural resources and regulatory inefficiencies that hinder the ease of doing business (OECD 2020b).

In the area of entrepreneurship, Kazakhstan has introduced mechanisms to stimulate SMEs, positioning them as a driver of economic diversification and job creation. Programs providing financial support, coupled with initiatives to promote sustainable business practices, have been pivotal to these efforts (Kazbekova et al. 2024). Despite these measures, entrepreneurs continue to face challenges in securing adequate funding, and gaps in entrepreneurial skills and education need to be addressed to unlock their full potential.

Promoting human capital development has been a cornerstone of Kazakhstan's economic strategy. Reforms in the education system aim to align with international standards and improve access to quality education, particularly in underserved regions (ADB 2018). Efforts to reduce regional disparities in educational and health care services further reinforce this objective. Nonetheless, the country continues to grapple with challenges such as brain drain, as skilled workers seek better opportunities abroad, and difficulties in ensuring consistent quality of education across its diverse regions.

Innovation and digitalization have been highlighted as critical components of economic modernization. Initiatives such as the establishment of technology parks, including the Astana Hub International Technology Park, and funding for early-stage start-ups reflect Kazakhstan's commitment to fostering a pro-innovation environment (OECD 2020b). However, barriers such as low digital literacy in rural areas and the need for substantial investments in digital infrastructure continue to limit the full potential of these efforts (Nakispekova 2024).

Finally, the government has sought to reduce regional inequalities through targeted development policies focusing on infrastructure improvement and equitable resource allocation (World Bank 2024c). Support for rural areas has included improved access to services and economic opportunities. Despite these initiatives, significant disparities in infrastructure and inefficiencies in resource distribution remain ongoing challenges to achieving balanced regional development. Although fiscal decentralization is not formally included as one of the five strategic pillars of Kazakhstan's National Development Plan, nor is the empowerment of subnational governments in financial matters, several elements of the Plan align with decentralization principles. In particular, the objectives of reducing territorial disparities, enhancing the quality of governance, and fostering inclusive regional development implicitly call for greater empowerment of subnational institutions. While the Plan does not explicitly propose greater budgetary autonomy for local governments, ongoing policy dialogues suggest growing recognition that achieving these national goals may benefit from targeted reforms to improve the fiscal and institutional capacity of local authorities. Accordingly, fiscal decentralization can be viewed as a complementary policy lever to support the broader implementation of the Plan.

The Middle-Income Trap in Kazakhstan

Beyond the challenges of diversifying its economy away from hydrocarbons, Kazakhstan faces the significant risk of falling into the "middle-income trap." This phenomenon occurs when countries experience rapid growth to reach middle-income status but struggle to transition to high-income levels (Kharas and Kohli 2011). Table 1 summarizes the key growth bottlenecks that middle-income countries typically encounter when trapped at this stage of development.

Kazakhstan aims to achieve high-income status and to double GDP by 2029, necessitating an average annual growth rate of 6 percentage points (Satubaldina 2023). However, sustaining this level of growth has become increasingly elusive. The 2024 World Bank World Development Report identifies several critical bottlenecks that threaten to push Kazakhstan toward economic stagnation (World Bank 2024b).

One important challenge is the dominance of a small number of large corporations, resulting in significant market concentration. This stifles fair competition and hampers productivity growth (World Bank 2024b).

Table 1: Middle-Income Trap: Summary of Main Bottlenecks

Growth Area	Factors	Bottlenecks
Economy	Slowing productivity growth	In many middle-income countries, growth is initially driven by low-wage, labor-intensive industries and resource extraction. As wages rise and natural resources become fully exploited, countries may struggle to maintain competitiveness without significant gains in productivity.
	Dependence on low-cost labor and natural resources	As labor costs rise and global demand for certain resources fluctuates, these countries can find themselves unable to compete with low-income countries (with cheaper labor) or high-income countries (with advanced technologies).
	Limited domestic demand growth	As growth slows, middle-income countries may face limited expansion in domestic demand, especially if income disparities prevent large portions of the population from increasing consumption.
	Rising inequality and regional disparities	These inequalities can lead to social tensions, discourage broad-based economic development, and make it challenging to maintain social and political stability, which are crucial for sustained growth.
Innovation	Limited innovation and technological advancement	Trapped countries may lack the infrastructure, investment, or institutional support for research and development, which prevents them from competing in knowledge-intensive sectors and developing unique, competitive products.
	Shift from investment-led to innovation-led growth	Many middle-income countries rely on investment-led growth, with a focus on infrastructure and physical capital. This approach provides diminishing returns over time and becomes less effective at higher levels of development.
Human capital	Inadequate human capital development	Insufficient investment in education, training, and skills development can leave middle-income countries without the highly skilled workforce necessary for moving into high-productivity industries.
Governance	Weak institutions and governance	Middle-income countries in the trap often have institutional weaknesses, such as corruption, bureaucratic inefficiency, and regulatory obstacles that stifle entrepreneurship and deter foreign investment.

Source: Authors' elaboration based on Kharas and Kohli (2011).

Additionally, restrictive product market regulations—commonly observed in middle-income countries—are pervasive in Kazakhstan. These include barriers to firm entry, licensing requirements, governance inefficiencies in state-owned enterprises, public procurement limitations, price controls, regulatory hurdles, and restrictions on foreign trade. Such regulations extend to network industries and services sectors, further curbing growth (World Bank 2024b). The substantial presence of publicly owned enterprises exacerbates these issues by limiting competition and hindering economic dynamism (World Bank 2024b).

Certain regions within Kazakhstan display characteristics indicative of the middle-income trap. While the national economy struggles to maintain past growth momentum, specific regions face more acute stagnation. Figure 6 shows the Development Trap Index for Kazakhstan's oblasts in 2023, assessing stagnation risk based on income levels, employment, and productivity trends (Rodríguez-Pose and Bartalucci 2021). Both high-income regions in the west and lagging regions in the south exhibit susceptibility to economic stagnation.

Figure 6: Development Trap Index Across Oblasts, 2023

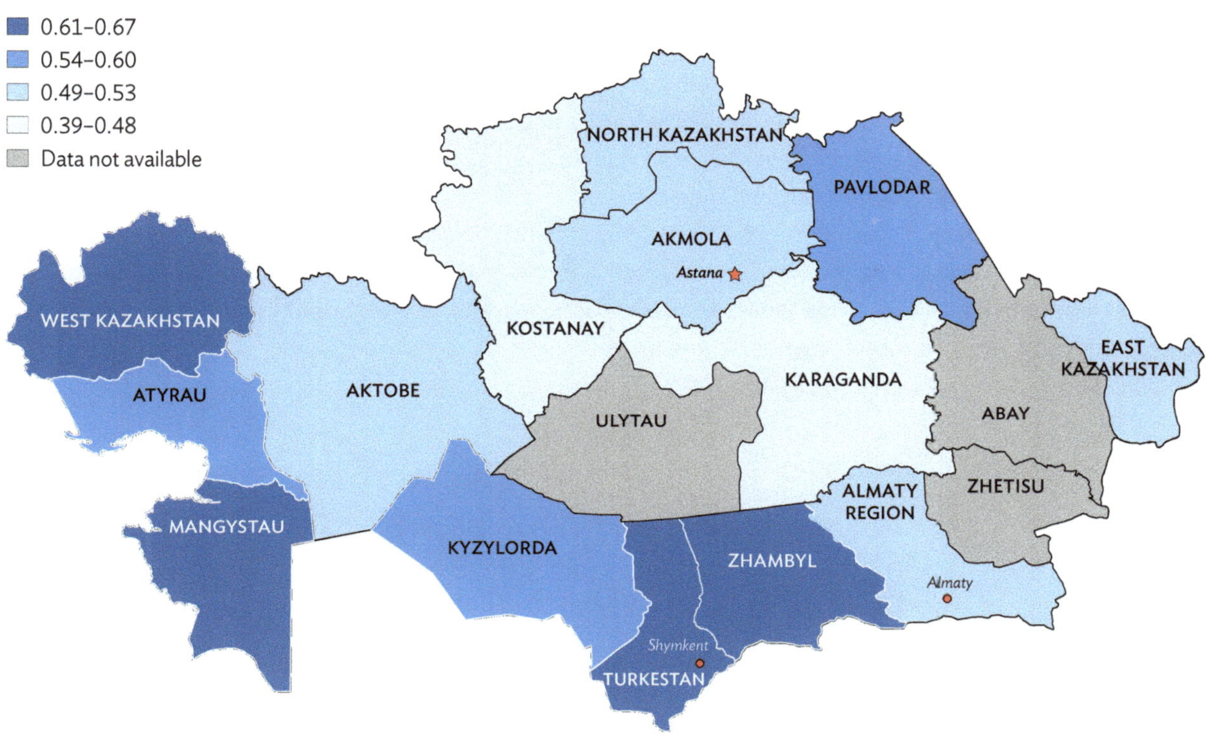

Source: Index based on Rodríguez-Pose and Bartalucci (2021) and updated by authors.

Kazakhstan's strategic goals are unlikely to be realized unless proactive reforms address these critical bottlenecks at both national and regional levels. Despite progress in areas such as education and economic frameworks, the economy's reliance on commodity exports and vulnerability to global market volatility remain pressing concerns. Furthermore, the concentration of economic activity in a few urban centers and regions risks suppressing growth and stifling dynamism across the broader economy.

The middle-income trap poses a substantial barrier to Kazakhstan's ambitions for sustained economic growth. The challenge of potentially entering a middle-income trap is not merely an issue of diminished productivity growth at the national level. It also has a distinct regional dimension. Across Kazakhstan, evidence points to certain regions that are not just lagging but also at risk of stagnation owing to weaker economic diversification, lower skills bases, or subdued investment in knowledge-intensive industries. In turn, this risk undermines the country's broader growth ambitions and prospects for graduating to high-income status (Rodríguez-Pose et al. 2024a).

Well-designed fiscal decentralization can help a country break out of or avoid a middle-income trap by empowering subnational governments to respond more effectively to local development gaps. When local authorities—especially in lagging regions—have sufficient autonomy over revenues and expenditures, they are better equipped to invest in productivity-enhancing projects, fortify local infrastructure, and foster the emergence of knowledge-based industries. In tandem, a robust regional equalization scheme can channel resources toward those territories most at risk of stagnation, shoring up human capital development and helping stimulate inward investment.

Nevertheless, the relationship between decentralization and a middle-income trap is not automatic. Devolved powers must be accompanied by adequate administrative capacity, transparency, and accountability at the subnational level to ensure newly delegated resources are used productively. Likewise, regional equalization must be carefully calibrated to tackle structural weaknesses—such as lack of innovation ecosystems or the adverse effects of resource dependence—without creating long-term reliance on transfers. By aligning fiscal decentralization and equalization strategies with the national effort to avert a middle-income trap, Kazakhstan can enhance the prospects for balanced economic development and resilience, ensuring no region remains locked in stagnation and the country progresses more confidently toward high-income status. Yet, this requires targeted reforms that stimulate innovation and enhance institutional effectiveness. These measures are essential for attracting investment into diverse industries and ensuring long-term economic resilience and growth.

CREATING ECOSYSTEMS FOR INNOVATION AND GROWTH 3

Kazakhstan's growth ambitions are bold, requiring the country to navigate an increasingly competitive global environment while contending with other fast-growing economies and developed nations. One of Kazakhstan's primary objectives is to enhance the competitiveness of its economic actors in a fundamentally interdependent world. Given the country's history, economic structure, and social model, achieving this goal by reducing labor and production costs or cutting workers' rights is not a viable path. Instead, for Kazakhstan to maintain and improve its global standing, an alternative approach is essential. It has to be one centered on innovation rather than low-cost labor. Enhancing competitiveness while preserving the country's social model requires moving up the technological and innovation scale.

At present, competitiveness within Kazakhstan is concentrated in urban areas and wealthier oblasts, as shown by the scores from the Regional Competitiveness and Cohesion Index across the country's oblasts (Figure 7). This index incorporates variables related to basic living standards, efficiency indicators, and innovation metrics. Table 2 ranks the oblasts based on normalized scores. The findings reveal that the most dynamic and competitive regions are the resource-rich western oblasts of Atyrau and Mangystau, along with the urban agglomerations of Astana and Almaty city. Conversely, the southern oblasts consistently perform the worst across the country.

Figure 7: Regional Competitiveness and Cohesion Index Across Oblasts, 2023

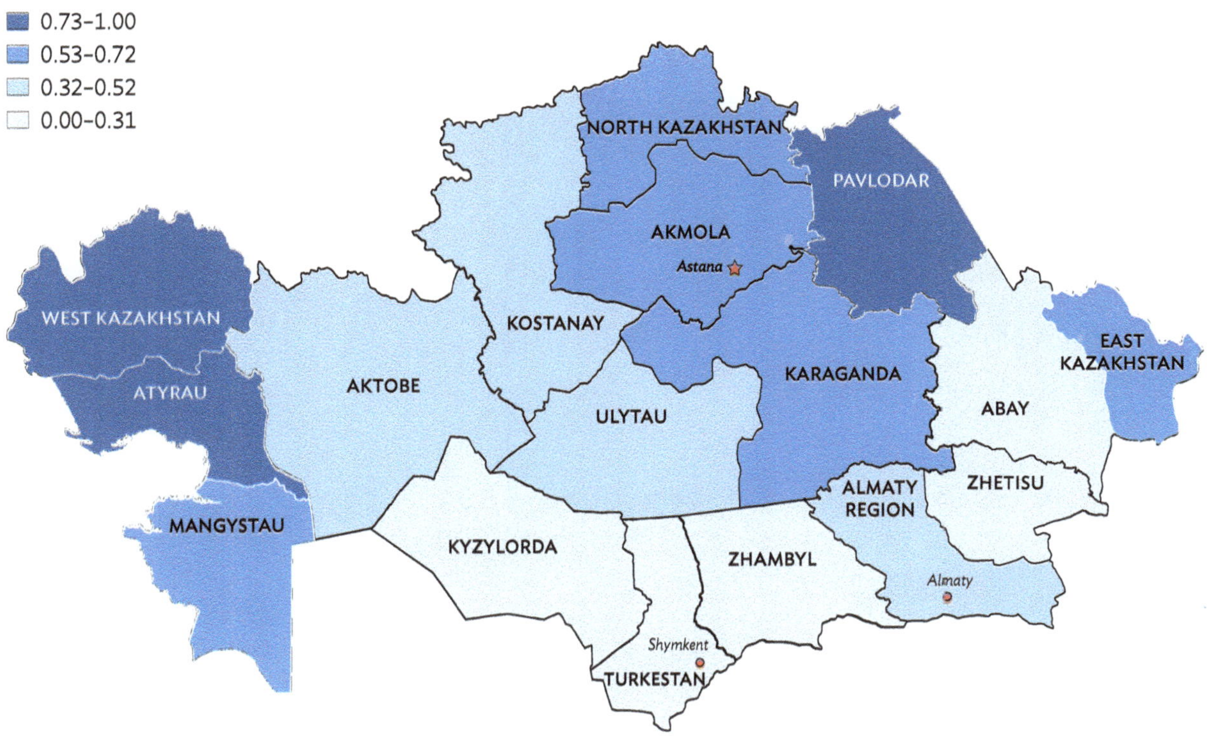

Source: Index based on Rodríguez-Pose and Bartalucci (2021) and updated by authors.

Table 2: Regional Ranking According to Normalized Scores of Regional Competitiveness and Cohesion Index, 2023

Rank	Region	Score
1	Almaty city	1.00
2	Atyrau	0.95
3	Astana city	0.89
4	West Kazakhstan	0.74
5	Pavlodar	0.73
6	Karaganda	0.72
7	Mangystau	0.67
8	East Kazakhstan	0.60
9	North Kazakhstan	0.59
10	Akmola	0.53
11	Kostanay	0.52
12	Aktobe	0.45
13	Shymkent city	0.44
14	Almaty	0.33
15	Ulytau	0.32
16	Abay	0.28
17	Kyzylorda	0.26
18	Zhambyl	0.15
19	Turkestan	0.11
20	Zhetisu	0.00

Notes: Regions color coded by quartiles, from dark green (highest) to dark orange (lowest). Scores are standardized for interpretation.

Source: Authors' elaboration based on data sourced from the Bureau of National Statistics of the Agency for Strategic Planning and Reforms of the Republic of Kazakhstan.

Competitiveness inequality is stark across numerous indicators. Substantial disparities exist in human capital across regions, gender, and socioeconomic status (World Bank 2021). For instance, a child born into the wealthiest 20% of households in Kazakhstan can expect to achieve 64% of their productivity potential, compared to just 53% for a child from the poorest 20% (World Bank 2021). These regional disparities are particularly evident in learning outcomes. Atyrau's Human Capital Index score aligns with much poorer countries like Kosovo and Georgia, whereas Astana's score approaches those of Luxembourg and the United States (World Bank 2021).

Quality of and expenditure on education also vary significantly across regions (World Bank 2021). Existing policies and funding structures often disincentivize teachers and school leaders from prioritizing low-achieving students. Similarly, despite ongoing health reforms, Kazakhstan exhibits considerable gaps compared to OECD countries in areas such as quality control of risk factors, health care delivery, and equitable expenditure across regions (World Bank 2021).

These disparities hinder growth and pose a risk to Kazakhstan's socioeconomic ambitions over the next decade. In this context, creating regional innovation ecosystems is critical to ensuring all regions contribute to national development. While research and development (R&D) is often considered the primary driver of innovation, other factors are equally essential in creating environments conducive to innovation, productivity, and sustainable development. Figure 8 presents a schematic representation of territorial development strategies designed to foster innovation and economic dynamism.

Figure 8: Schematic Representation of Territorial Development Strategies

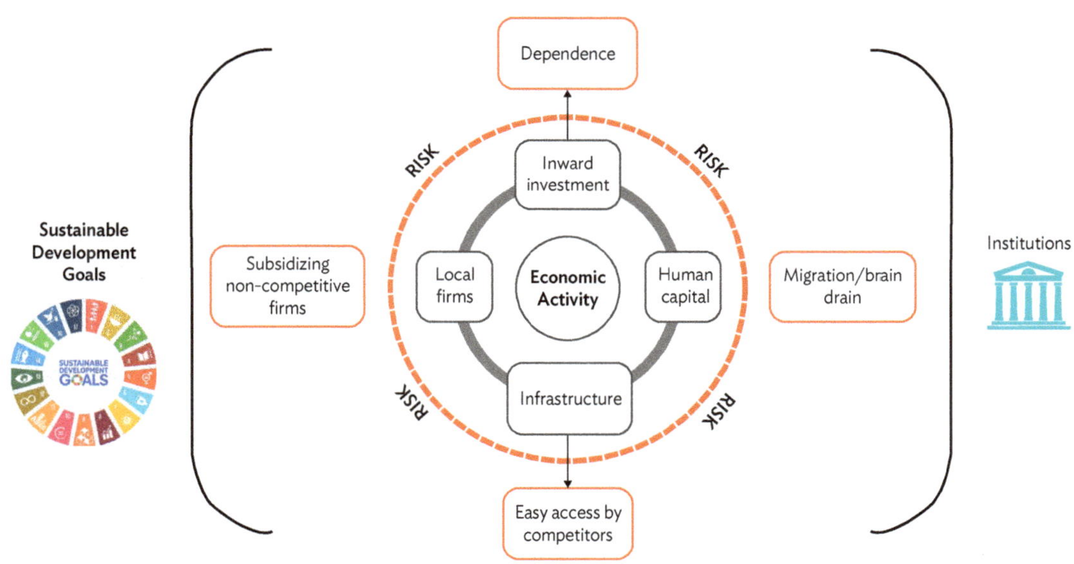

Source: Authors' elaboration adapted from Rodríguez-Pose (2002).

The model highlights key components and potential risks associated with territorial development strategies that prioritize innovation. Applied to Kazakhstan, the framework emphasizes balancing local and international investments, addressing structural risks, and aligning development efforts with the Sustainable Development Goals (SDGs). At the heart of the model is economic activity, driven by four interconnected elements: inward investment, human capital, infrastructure, and local firms.

Inward investment brings capital, expertise, and innovation to regions, while human capital development ensures a skilled and knowledgeable workforce. Physical and digital infrastructure supports businesses and enhances connectivity, facilitating both regional and global integration. Empowering local firms allows them to remain competitive in domestic and international markets, further propelling economic growth.

However, several risks must be managed. Heavy reliance on foreign investors can create economic vulnerabilities, especially if investments remain concentrated in extractive industries. Diversifying the economy is essential to mitigate this dependence. Brain drain poses another significant challenge, as the migration of skilled workers undermines local innovation and economic potential. Attracting and retaining talent requires competitive opportunities, improved living standards, and a supportive environment for workers.

Subsidizing noncompetitive firms can stifle growth, while market liberalization without safeguards may harm domestic industries. Strong institutions are critical for ensuring effective governance, transparent policies, and robust investment in R&D.

Aligning development efforts with the SDGs, such as promoting quality education, decent work, and reduced inequalities, ensures growth is inclusive and sustainable. Leveraging Kazakhstan's strategic position as a transit hub, advancing education reforms, and fostering innovation in non-resource sectors, such as technology and agriculture, are vital for achieving long-term economic resilience and sustainable growth.

FISCAL DECENTRALIZATION AS A MECHANISM FOR GROWTH

4

Taxation is key in delivering more equitable economic development in Kazakhstan.[2] Progressive taxation, in particular, can significantly reduce regional inequalities by ensuring a more balanced distribution of resources across the country. Such measures drive economic growth and enhance public services for all citizens (OECD 2023a). Taxes and their revenues can support both economic growth and regional balance through a variety of mechanisms.

In this report, we draw on a broad definition of fiscal decentralization. The economic rationale behind fiscal decentralization often centers on efficiency gains, as local governments—when adequately empowered—may allocate resources in closer alignment with local preferences and needs. This is reflected in measures of subnational budgetary autonomy on the expenditure side, as well as in the degree of political and administrative authority local governments exercise over the provision of services.

In particular, many definitions of fiscal decentralization emphasize that local populations benefit when elected local governments can levy taxes (or receive a share of national taxes) and determine local spending priorities. Although this report devotes considerable attention to the issue of tax devolution—as it has critical implications for enhancing local revenue bases and accountability—this focus should not be interpreted as equating "fiscal decentralization" solely with "tax devolution." Rather, the potential efficiency and accountability gains derived from empowering local governments on the expenditure side, ensuring strong political representation, and improving administrative capacity are equally integral to a successful decentralization process. Strengthening local institutions and improving subnational governance are thus key elements of fiscal decentralization and must go hand in hand with any reforms designed to devolve taxing authority.

Progressive tax policies generate revenue that can be used to fund fiscal transfers from wealthier to less-developed regions. These transfers finance critical infrastructure, health care, education, and other essential services, enabling the entire country—and particularly its less prosperous areas—to improve socioeconomic standards (OECD 2023a). Tax incentives, including reduced corporate tax rates, tax holidays, and business credits, can encourage companies to invest in economically vulnerable regions, creating jobs and stimulating local economies. Additionally, property and land taxes provide local governments with a means to generate independent revenue, reducing their reliance on national transfers. This autonomy allows investments in projects tailored to specific community needs. Similarly, targeted tax credits or reductions in personal income taxes for professionals working in underserved areas can mitigate brain drain by incentivizing skilled workers to contribute to local economies (OECD 2023a).

[2] Fiscal decentralization often includes a plethora of functions to be transferred to subnational governments. In this report, we focus mainly on tax devolution as a way to strengthen subnational financial autonomy and accountability.

That said, the positive impact exerted by progressive tax policies is contingent on several factors. The effectiveness of fiscal transfers and tax incentives depends on how the grants are distributed, the expenditure responsibilities assigned to local governments, and the willingness of subnational governments to adequately tax themselves. Without proper allocation and strong local governance, the potential for socioeconomic improvements in less-developed regions could be limited (World Bank 2021). Moreover, the success of tax incentives relies heavily on the proper targeting of economically vulnerable areas and the long-term commitment of businesses to invest in those regions.

Moreover, whereas tax devolution is often an important component of fiscal decentralization, expenditure decentralization can also bring about non-negligible efficiency gains (World Bank 2021). In particular, expenditure decentralization involves empowering local governments with the authority to allocate resources for public services based on the needs and preferences of their communities. This allows local governments to tailor services such as health care, education, and infrastructure to regional priorities, enhancing the efficiency and effectiveness of public service delivery. Local governments are thus better positioned to address specific local challenges, leading to improvements in both the quality and the accessibility of services, particularly in regions with diverse socioeconomic conditions (World Bank 2021).

Research shows that expenditure decentralization can drive economic efficiency gains, as local governments are typically more familiar with the needs of their constituents and can prioritize spending where it has the greatest impact (World Bank 2021). In Kazakhstan, with its wide regional disparities, decentralizing expenditure could help bridge gaps in infrastructure and services between urban and rural areas, fostering more balanced and inclusive development. Local governments, being closer to the population, can allocate resources more effectively than a centralized system that may not fully capture local needs (Allain-Dupre, Chatry, and Moisio 2020).

Figure 9 illustrates the four conceptual pillars usually believed to make up fiscal decentralization: expenditure assignment, revenue assignment, intergovernmental fiscal transfers, and local government borrowing and debt management. Whereas this report mainly focuses on revenue assignment—that is, tax devolution—and fiscal transfers from the central to local governments, various sections of the report discuss the implications of devolution of expenditure responsibilities.

Figure 9: Schematic Representation of the Four Pillars Associated with Fiscal Decentralization

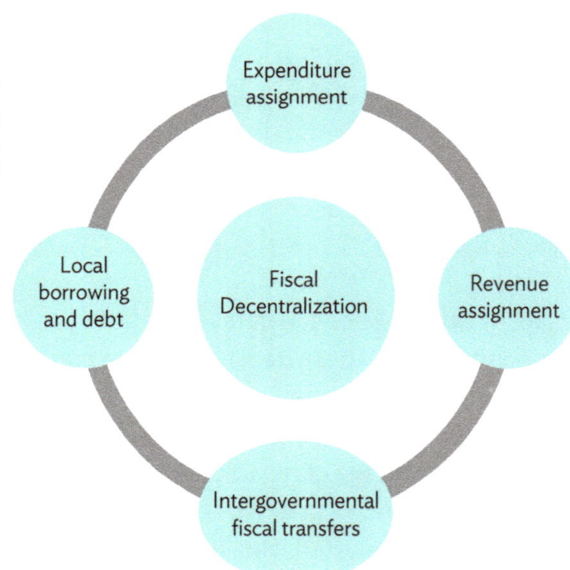

Source: Authors' elaboration based on World Bank (2021).

Kazakhstan and Its Revenue Collection Challenges

Kazakhstan has long grappled with challenges related to low tax revenues. Fiscal capacity at both the central and the subnational levels remains well below potential, particularly when compared to OECD averages. Although tax revenues have increased over the past decade, their share of GDP has declined and remains far below global benchmarks (OECD 2020a). In 2023, Kazakhstan's tax revenue amounted to approximately 11% of its GDP, significantly below the OECD average of 34% (OECD 2023b).

The country's tax revenues are not only limited but also undiversified and volatile by international standards. Kazakhstan's tax structure relies heavily on value-added tax (VAT) and corporate income tax (CIT), with relatively minor contributions from personal income tax (PIT), social security contributions, and property taxes. This dependence on VAT and CIT revenues from a small number of large companies within limited sectors results in a narrow tax base, exposing the country to heightened revenue volatility. Even when compared to other resource-rich OECD nations and emerging economies, Kazakhstan's reliance on a few industries amplifies its fiscal vulnerability (OECD 2020a).

Major revenue sources, such as CIT and export duties on crude oil, are concentrated in the mining and fossil fuel sectors, making CIT revenues highly susceptible to fluctuations in global oil prices. Similarly, VAT revenue volatility has increased in recent years, exacerbating fiscal instability.

At the subnational level, similar challenges persist. While the share of subnational revenues and expenditures in Kazakhstan's GDP has increased slightly over the past 3 years—by 1% and 0.5%, respectively—fiscal capacity at the subnational level remains low in relation to gross regional product (GRP) and oblast populations (Figure 10).

Figure 10: Share of Subnational Revenues and Expenditure of Country's Gross Domestic Product, 2021–2023

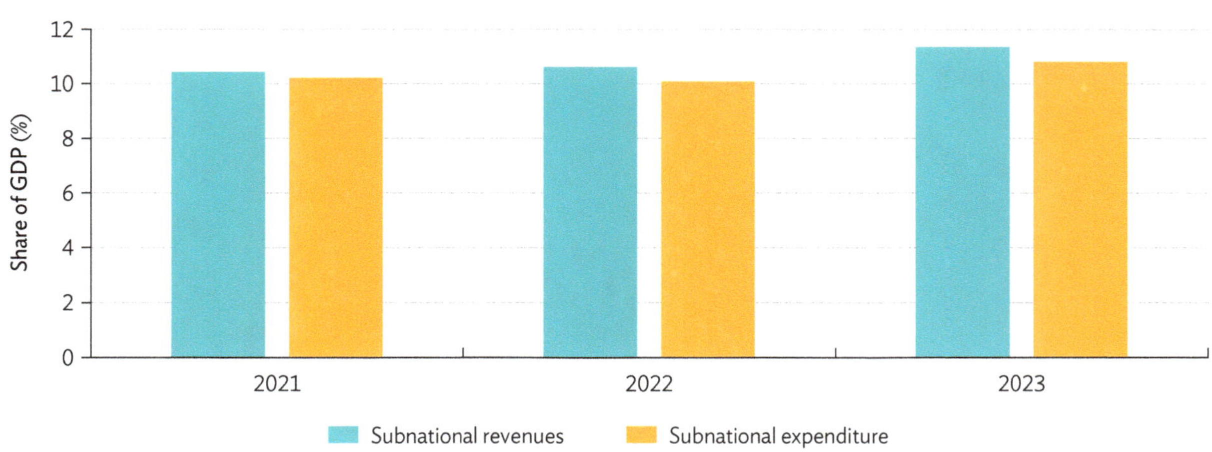

GDP = gross domestic product.

Source: Authors' elaboration based on data from the Bureau of National Statistics of the Agency for Strategic Planning and Reforms of the Republic of Kazakhstan.

Figures 11 and 12 depict fiscal capacity across Kazakhstan's oblasts, measured by GRP and population for 2023. Certain oblasts, including Kyzylorda, Abay, Turkestan, and Zhetisu, demonstrate low fiscal capacity on both metrics. Conversely, oblasts such as Pavlodar, Almaty, Astana, and Atyrau exhibit substantially higher fiscal capacity. Despite these regional variations, fiscal capacity across all oblasts remains limited, with tax revenues ranging from 7.5% of GRP in Almaty city to as low as 3.3% in West Kazakhstan.

Figure 11: Subnational Tax Revenues as a Percentage of Oblasts' Gross Regional Product, 2023

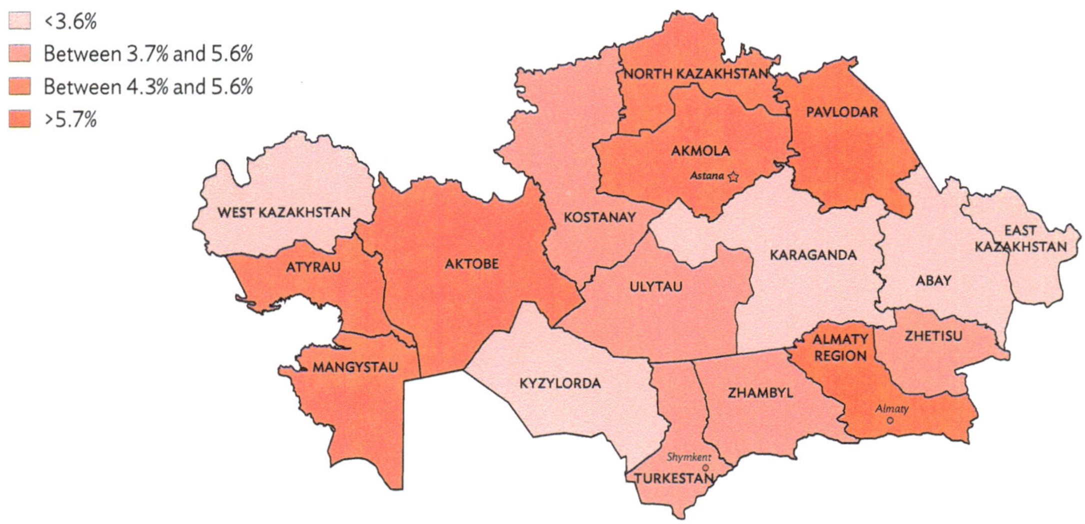

Source: Authors' elaboration based on data from the Bureau of National Statistics of the Agency for Strategic Planning and Reforms of the Republic of Kazakhstan.

Figure 12: Tax Revenues as a Share of Oblasts' Population, 2023

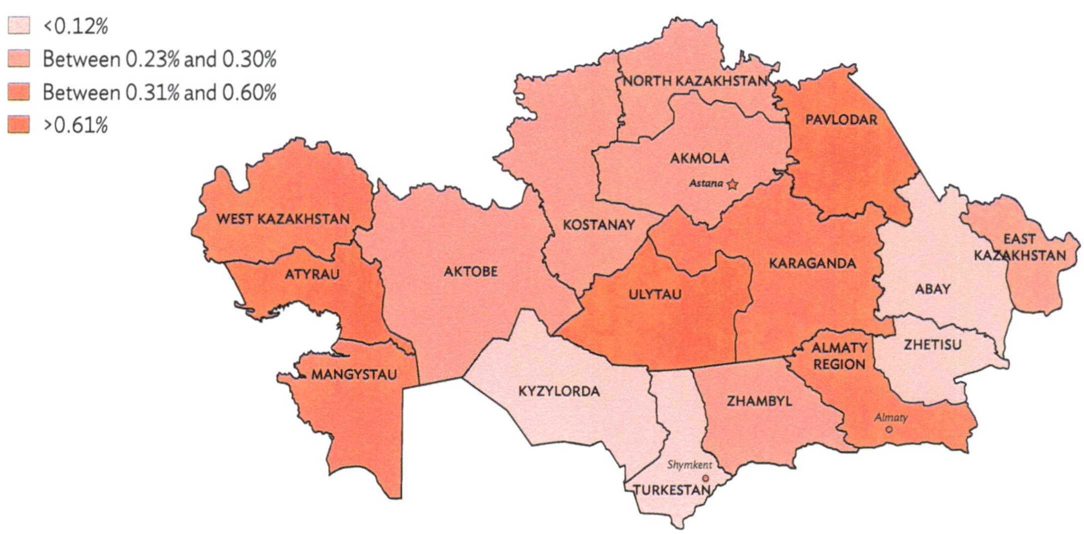

Source: Authors' elaboration based on data from the Bureau of National Statistics of the Agency for Strategic Planning and Reforms of the Republic of Kazakhstan.

Finally, Figure 13 reports the shares of subnational government expenditure and revenues in 2023. As can be observed, the largest share of both expenditure and revenues is a direct responsibility of the central government, with only around 40% of revenues in the hands of subnational governments (oblasts) and roughly 30% of total expenditure.

Figure 13: Share of Subnational and National Government Out of Total Government Revenues and Expenditure

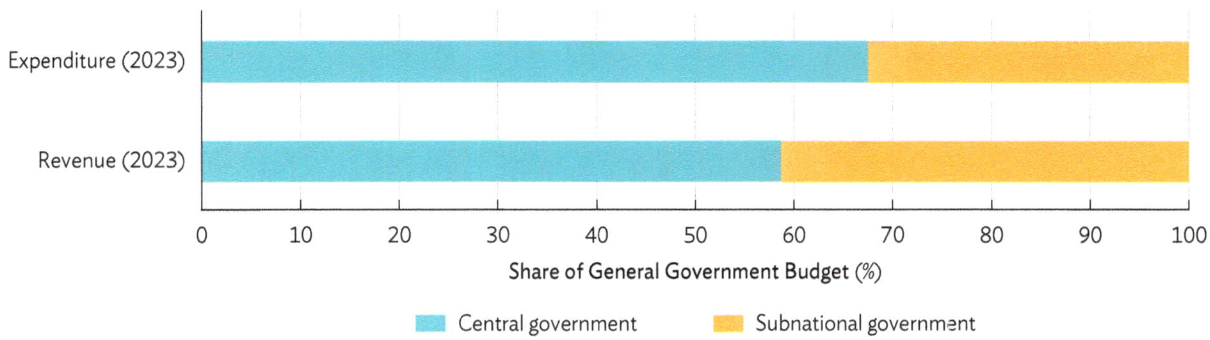

Source: Authors' elaboration based on data from the Bureau of National Statistics of the Agency for Strategic Planning and Reforms of the Republic of Kazakhstan.

Figure 14 shows the revenue structure of local budgets of Kazakhstan for 2021–2023.

Figure 14: Revenue Structure of Local Budgets of Kazakhstan for 2021–2023

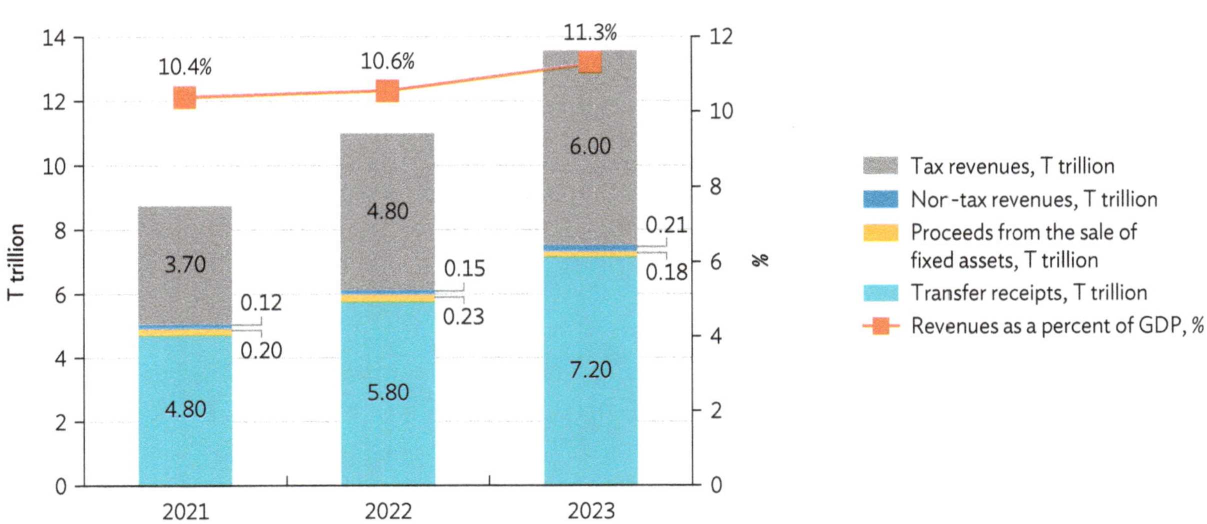

GDP = gross domestic product.

Source: Authors' elaboration based on data from the Ministry of Finance of the Republic of Kazakhstan and the Bureau of National Statistics of the Agency for Strategic Planning and Reforms of the Republic of Kazakhstan.

Revenues of local budgets of Kazakhstan for the period 2021–2023 increased by 55.0%—from T8.7 trillion (10.4% of GDP) in 2021 to T13.6 trillion (11.3% of GDP) in 2023.

In the structure of local budget revenues, the largest share is made up of transfer receipts, which contribute an average of 53.3% over the analyzed period. They increased 1.5 times: from T4.8 trillion (5.7% of GDP) in 2021 to T7.2 trillion (6.0% of GDP) in 2023.

Tax revenues for 2021–2023 accounted for an average of 43.4% of all local budget revenues. These revenues increased 1.6 times, from T3.7 trillion (4.4% of GDP) in 2021 to T6.0 trillion (5.0% of GDP) in 2023.

The most dependent regions are Zhetisu region (the share of transfer receipts in revenues of the budget of the region in 2022 was 93.5%; in 2023 it was 83.6%) and Turkestan region (in 2021 [86.4%], in 2022 [85.0%], in 2023 [86.3%]). The regions least dependent on transfer receipts are Atyrau region (in 2021 [15.3%], in 2022 [18.2%], in 2023 [9.7%]) and Almaty city (in 2021 [17.4%], in 2022 [16.0%], in 2023 [7.7%]).

Proceeds from the sale of fixed assets contributed to local budget revenues by an average of 1.9% over the period analyzed. They decreased by 10.3 from T0.2 trillion (0.24% of GDP) in 2021 to T0.18 trillion (0.15% of GDP) in 2023.

Nontax revenues accounted for the smallest share in the revenue structure of local budgets, for an average of 1.4% of all revenues. This type of revenue increased 1.7 times, from T0.12 trillion (0.14% of GDP) in 2021 to T0.18 trillion (0.17% of GDP) in 2023.

The ability of regions to resolve issues related to the socioeconomic development of the territory at the expense of their own financial resources depends on the amount of tax revenue, which is one of the most important sources of income for local budgets.

Tax revenues collected from the region go to the republican budget and the regional budget, the budgets of the city of republican significance, and the capital, and, therefore, tax collection in the regional budget becomes less, which reduces the size of its own financial resources.

In 2021–2023, tax revenues to the republican budget from only three regions—Zhambyl region, North Kazakhstan region, and Shymkent city—were less than tax revenues to the corresponding local budgets. Tax revenues from all other regions to the republican budget exceeded tax revenues to the corresponding local budgets.

The largest share of tax revenues to the republican budget was taken by tax revenues collected from Almaty city (29.4% of all tax revenues to the republican budget in 2021, 29.4% in 2022, 30.7% in 2023), Atyrau region (15.6% in 2021, 17.8% in 2022, 15.4% in 2023), and Astana city (10.9% in 2021, 11.7% in 2022, 13.9% in 2023). The smallest share of tax revenues to the republican budget comprised tax revenues collected from North Kazakhstan region (0.7% of all tax revenues to the republican budget in 2021, 0.5% in 2022, 0.6% in 2023) and Zhambyl region (0.6% in 2021, 0.6% in 2022, 0.5% in 2023).

Fiscal Decentralization for Revenue Enhancement

Considering Kazakhstan's historically low tax revenues, the government is pursuing a series of tax reforms aimed at broadening the tax base and improving compliance. Among the key priorities in the new tax code are the adoption of digital tax systems and measures to combat tax evasion. Alongside these initiatives, fiscal decentralization is increasingly recognized as a mechanism for enhancing revenue collection. Fiscal decentralization entails delegating taxing and spending authority from the central government to regional or local governments. This approach can promote greater local accountability, responsiveness to regional needs, and competition between regions, potentially leading to more efficient public service delivery (Martínez-Vázquez, Lago Peñas, and Sacchi 2017).

Although fiscal decentralization is not a universal solution, it holds significant potential to foster more equitable economic growth under appropriate conditions. Research indicates that its success depends on various factors, including institutional quality, existing regional disparities, and the country's level of development (Farole, Rodriguez-Pose, and Storper 2011; Sepúlveda and Martínez-Vázquez 2011; Martínez-Vázquez, Lago Peñas, and Sacchi 2017). Table 3 summarizes the benefits and risks associated with fiscal decentralization.

Table 3: Benefits and Risks of Fiscal Decentralization

Aspect	Benefits	Risks
Local knowledge and efficiency	□ Better alignment of public services with local preferences	□ Local governments may lack capacity to efficiently manage resources
	□ Enhanced efficiency in resource allocation	□ Potential inefficiencies if local authorities are not well equipped
Regional competition and economic growth	□ Encourages competition among regions to attract business and investment	□ Competition may trigger a race to the bottom in tax rates, reducing public revenues
	□ Stimulates innovation and economic dynamism	□ Risk of exacerbating regional inequalities as wealthier regions attract more investment
Governance and accountability	□ Greater accountability as local governments are closer to the population	□ Increased risk of corruption and misuse of funds
	□ Promotes responsiveness to local needs and demands	□ May lead to fragmentation and inefficiency in service delivery if poorly coordinated

Sources: Authors' elaboration based on Prud'homme (1995), Besley and Burgess (2002), Martínez-Vázquez and McNab (2003), Ezcurra and Pascual (2008), Rodríguez-Pose and Ezcurra (2010), Baskaran and Feld (2013), Lessman and Markwardt (2016), Kyriacou et al. (2017), Martínez-Vázquez et al. (2017), Rodríguez-Pose and Ketterer (2020).

Experiences of fiscal decentralization across the world provide compelling insights into the potential of fiscal decentralization to drive localized economic growth, foster innovation, and reduce disparities. In particular, the cases of Brazil, the People's Republic of China (PRC), and Germany show how fiscal decentralization can be used as a tool for promoting inclusive economic development, as Appendix 1 indicates. Brazil's approach also points to the capacity of fiscal decentralization to enhance welfare and support regional economic development. The country's framework, established by the 1988 Constitution, grants states and municipalities significant autonomy over revenue generation and spending, enabling the implementation of innovative social programs like *Bolsa Família* and sustainable development initiatives in the Amazon region.

Similarly, the PRC's decentralized system, characterized by revenue sharing and regional autonomy in policy implementation, has spurred remarkable economic growth and innovation. By empowering local governments to experiment with policies, attract investment, and issue bonds for infrastructure projects, the PRC has facilitated regional transformations, such as Shenzhen's rise as a global technology hub and Jiangsu's leadership in renewable energy production.

Germany's federal system demonstrates how shared tax revenues, robust equalization mechanisms, and fiscal autonomy for regional governments can promote balanced economic development while ensuring comparable living standards across regions. The Länders'—federal regions'—ability to tailor policies to local needs, supported by fiscal equalization mechanisms like the *Länderfinanzausgleich* and strict debt regulations, has contributed to regional resilience and national stability.

However, the case studies in Appendix 1 also underscore the risks associated with fiscal decentralization, such as exacerbated regional inequalities in the PRC and Brazil, and reduced incentives for economically stronger regions to generate revenue in Germany. These experiences emphasize the need for robust equalization mechanisms, transparent governance, and a balance between regional autonomy and national cohesion to maximize the benefits of fiscal decentralization while addressing its challenges.

KAZAKHSTAN'S MOVE TOWARD FISCAL DECENTRALIZATION 5

Kazakhstan's Local Institutional Arrangements and Fiscal Decentralization

Kazakhstan's subnational government structure consists of three main levels: regions (oblasts), districts (raions), and local municipalities (cities, towns, and villages). While local elections are held for representative bodies known as *maslikhats*, key executive officials such as regional and district *akims* (governors and mayors) are appointed rather than directly elected by the local population. The President of Kazakhstan appoints oblast *akims*, while district and city *akims* are appointed by higher-level authorities, often in consultation with the central government. This system ensures strong central oversight but limits the direct electoral accountability of executive local officials to the residents they serve (OECD 2017).

Accountability arrangements in Kazakhstan are structured to ensure oversight from both local representative bodies and the central government. *Maslikhats,* which are elected by local populations, serve as advisory and legislative bodies that approve regional and local development plans, but their powers are limited in practice. The appointed *akims*, who execute policies and budgets, report primarily to the central government rather than to *maslikhats* (OECD 2017). While citizens can participate in public consultations and provide feedback, the ultimate decision-making power remains concentrated at higher administrative levels. Additionally, the central government can remove local officials if they fail to meet national policy objectives, reinforcing a hierarchical governance structure (OECD 2020b).

Budget formulation and execution at the subnational level require approval from central authorities, particularly for significant expenditures. Local governments prepare budgets based on anticipated revenues, but these budgets must align with national priorities and financial regulations. While local *maslikhats* formally approve their respective budgets, they operate within constraints set by the Ministry of Finance (MOF) and higher-tier government bodies (OECD 2017). Central government approval is necessary for budgetary allocations, particularly for projects involving infrastructure, education, health care, and social services (OECD 2020b). Additionally, fiscal transfers from the central government, which constitute a significant portion of local budgets, often come with earmarked spending requirements, further limiting local discretion in financial matters.

In terms of expenditure responsibilities, subnational governments are tasked with delivering key public services including education, health care, housing, and local infrastructure. However, the discretion they hold over both the formation and the execution of budgets is limited. Budget proposals must align with national policy objectives and are subject to approval by MOF and other central authorities. Central government transfers, which constitute a significant share of subnational budgets, are often earmarked and come with strict spending conditions.

Despite some flexibility in managing day-to-day expenditures, subnational governments in Kazakhstan remain financially dependent on the central government (OECD 2020b). While they generate some revenue through local taxes such as property and land taxes, these funds are generally insufficient to cover regional needs. The central government provides substantial financial support through intergovernmental transfers, including equalization grants to balance disparities between wealthier and poorer regions. However, since these funds are often designated for specific purposes, local authorities have limited autonomy in setting independent fiscal priorities. As a result, while Kazakhstan has a structured subnational governance system, its financial and administrative decision making remains highly centralized, with key budgetary and policy decisions ultimately controlled by the national government (OECD 2017).

Kazakhstan has been actively pursuing fiscal decentralization to enhance the financial independence of local budgets. Key measures in this process include redistributing tax revenues to regional and local governments, enabling them to fund local infrastructure, social services, and economic development projects more effectively. Between 2020 and 2023, several significant reforms were introduced to expand the revenue base of local budgets. Under the Concept for the Development of Local Self-Government until 2030, 25 types of taxes and payments were transferred to the fourth level of the budget to strengthen the financial autonomy of rural districts. These include PIT, personal property tax, land tax, vehicle tax, fees for outdoor advertising, and the unified land tax, among others. Additionally, in 2020, CIT from SMEs was allocated to local budgets, further enhancing their financial independence.

The new Budget Code—currently under review by Kazakhstan's Parliament—proposes additional tax revenue redistribution to improve financial stability at the local level. One of its key measures involves transferring mineral extraction tax on common minerals, groundwater, and therapeutic mud from the national budget to local budgets. This reform ensures that cities of republican significance, regional centers, districts, and rural areas benefit directly from local resource extraction activities.

Additionally, tax revenues generated from specially protected natural areas will be distributed based on their significance. Fees collected from national-level protected areas will be directed to the republican budget, while those from locally significant areas will be allocated to regional and municipal budgets. Similarly, revenues from payments for the use of plant resources will be distributed not only to regional budgets but also to the budgets of major cities and the capital.

Another reform involves reallocating unified land tax revenues from city budgets to district budgets, ensuring a fairer distribution of financial resources at the local level. Payments for negative environmental impacts have also been reclassified as special income rather than tax revenue, allowing these funds to be used more effectively for environmental initiatives. Collectively, these fiscal decentralization measures aim to strengthen the financial autonomy of local governments, optimize resource allocation, and support regional economic growth. By ensuring tax revenues generated within a region remain there, Kazakhstan is advancing a more balanced and sustainable approach to local governance and development.

In Kazakhstan, CIT and VAT rates are set at the central level. However, in recent years, measures have been introduced to stimulate specific economic sectors through differentiated tax rates. The standard CIT rate is 20% for most enterprises, while a 0% rate applies to the social sector—including education, health care, and social services—to support these low-margin industries. Additionally, a 70% reduction in the CIT rate has been granted to the agriculture sector to encourage its development.

Under the new Tax Code, a reduced CIT rate of 10% has been introduced for the manufacturing industry to promote modernization, enhance competitiveness, and create new jobs. Meanwhile, VAT remains set at a universal 12% across all goods and services, serving as a primary source of indirect tax revenue for the national budget.

A significant step in fiscal decentralization was the 2020 reform, which allowed a portion of CIT revenue from SMEs to be transferred to local budgets. This initiative sought to enhance the financial independence of regional governments while stimulating local economic growth. The new Budget Code builds upon this by continuing to redistribute certain tax revenues, including CIT, between central and local governments, thereby granting local authorities greater financial management capabilities.

Despite these reforms, local authorities in Kazakhstan remain limited in their ability to introduce, modify, or regulate tax rates. However, they are authorized to determine rates in specific areas, including setting base rates for land within settlements, regulating fees for the use of surface water resources, and determining charges for forest and plant resource usage based on calculations provided by local executive bodies. Additionally, local governments may lower tax rates on industrial land, such as mines and quarries, and reduce taxes on land allocated for parking lots, petrol stations, or casinos if these properties are not used as intended or if legal violations occur.

These regulatory powers allow local governments to adjust taxation based on regional characteristics, reinforcing fiscal sustainability and promoting economic development. By managing tax rates within clearly defined areas and resources, local authorities gain essential tools to align taxation policies with local economic conditions and priorities, ensuring a more flexible and adaptive fiscal system.[3]

Kazakhstan has introduced several mechanisms to increase the financial autonomy of local authorities and promote local economic growth. A central component of this strategy is fiscal decentralization, which provides local governments with greater powers in taxation, enabling regions to adjust tax rates and develop policies that reflect their specific economic circumstances.

For instance, local authorities can modify land tax rates based on zoning schemes developed in accordance with national land legislation, with the ability to adjust these rates by up to 50% of the basic land tax rate.

[3] Subnational taxation tends to play a far greater role in the public finances of higher-income countries, with property taxes, local surcharges on personal income taxes, and various smaller levies forming a critical part of local government revenues. Conversely, in middle- and lower-income economies, local tax receipts usually constitute a more modest proportion of overall government revenues. This disparity is often linked to administrative constraints—where local authorities may lack the capacity or tools to collect taxes efficiently—and to structural factors such as significant reliance on central government transfers. Moreover, tax competition, whether across local jurisdictions or between central and regional levels of government, can also dampen subnational revenue collection.

In this regard, Kazakhstan has a profile that does not reflect its income level. Municipal or oblast-level taxation remain somewhat circumscribed by technical, administrative, and institutional limitations. As highlighted throughout this report, the authorities have enacted a series of deregulatory measures—effectively devolving certain taxes and fees to local governments—yet these steps have not automatically translated into higher local tax take. Achieving sustainable subnational revenues will require further strengthening of administrative capacity, the adoption of clearer data collection standards, and alignment between central and local tax policy to avoid excessive competition or duplication. Focusing on robust local taxes such as property levies and graduated income taxes remains a key avenue for expanding municipal fiscal space. Equally important, however, is designing intergovernmental transfers that do not undermine local revenue mobilization.

Similarly, for land occupied by housing stock, including buildings and structures, local governments can modify tax rates within the same range. Additionally, for outdoor advertising placed in public spaces, local authorities may increase basic monthly fees by up to two times, depending on location. Tax rates on industrial land, including mines and quarries, can be reduced by up to 30% of the base rate. Local governments also determine fees for the use of surface water resources and forest and plant resources and have the authority to lower the retail tax rate under the special tax regime.

By expanding fiscal decentralization, Kazakhstan is creating a more stable and predictable economic environment that attracts investment and stimulates business activity. Local authorities, with their in-depth understanding of regional economic and social needs, are now better positioned to implement tax policies that support sustainable growth. Strengthening the tax base ensures the long-term financial stability of regions while creating favorable conditions for economic development. The share of personal property tax within local budgets varies depending on income levels, economic development, and tax collection efficiency. In large cities and regional centers, this share is typically higher owing to the larger volume of real estate and higher property values.

Kazakhstan's New Tax Code

Kazakhstan has recently embarked on implementing a new Tax Code to address persistent challenges associated with low tax revenue collection, as discussed in earlier sections. This reform process, guided by presidential directives, seeks to improve efficiency, broaden the tax base, and encourage reinvestment in economic modernization. Key elements include the introduction of differentiated tax rates, reductions in CIT for profits reinvested into modernization, and the establishment of a "luxury tax."

The implementation time line for these reforms is structured around major milestones. By 1 September 2022, the government had aimed to reduce taxes and mandatory payments by 20%, cut tax benefits by 20%, transition to a service model for tax administration, and reduce the number of tax reporting forms by 30%. By 1 September 2023, the focus shifted to introducing incentives for reinvesting profits, adjusting special tax regimes, reforming VAT, developing transparent rules for tax benefits, and digitalizing tax administration processes. Additional reductions in taxes and mandatory payments were implemented in early 2024.

The new Tax Code consolidates taxes, fees, charges, and duties into a more streamlined structure. For example, it includes a unified land tax and revised fees for services such as outdoor advertising, licensing, and the registration of movable property pledges. A comprehensive review of tax benefits identified 744 points, of which 285 were deemed administrative clarifications rather than benefits, while 459 were identified as actual tax benefits. Approximately 20% of these benefits, valued at T1.3 trillion, is proposed for cancellation to ensure remaining tax benefits are better targeted and justified.

Notable changes introduced under the new tax regime include the following:

- **Corporate taxation:** Differentiated CIT rates now reflect the economic activities of various sectors. A flat rate of 20% applies uniformly across all of Kazakhstan. However, reduced rates are in place for specific sectors: 10% for manufacturing, a complete CIT waiver for the social sector, and a 70% reduction for the agriculture sector. Additionally, certain CIT revenues, such as those originating from SMEs, are now transferred to local budgets. These measures aim to support priority sectors while equitably distributing the tax burden.

- **Investment tax preferences:** To incentivize economic growth, the Tax Code allows for a 100% deduction of costs related to acquiring or constructing buildings, machinery, and software, provided these assets are used for at least 3 years. Taxpayers producing and selling their own products benefit from reduced CIT and PIT rates, while R&D expenses are eligible for deductions of up to 300%. Moreover, VAT on imported raw materials processed in Kazakhstan can be deferred for 1 year.
- **Personal taxation:** Reforms include PIT exemptions for pension payments, reduced vehicle tax rates based on vehicle age, higher property tax rates for high-value real estate, and increased excise taxes on luxury goods. These measures aim to create a fairer tax system for individuals while addressing wealth disparities.

While the new Tax Code introduces significant changes to national taxation, it does not include provisions for fiscal decentralization. Tax administration and revenue collection remain centralized under the national government. Nonetheless, the government has expressed its intention to pursue fiscal decentralization as a means of empowering local authorities, enhancing regional autonomy, and promoting balanced economic development.

Requirements for a Successful Fiscal Decentralization in Kazakhstan

Fiscal decentralization in Kazakhstan involves empowering local governments to raise and manage their own revenues, granting them greater autonomy in public spending. In practice, this entails policies ranging from providing flexibility over existing revenue sources to enabling local retention of national taxes or introducing entirely new local taxes. Below, we outline five key elements that—based on the benefits and risks of fiscal decentralization discussed in this and previous reports—can contribute to a more effective decentralization framework.

(a) Increased Flexibility over Existing Local Revenues and Expenditure Responsibilities

A foundational step toward fiscal decentralization is granting local governments greater control over their existing revenue sources, particularly property and land taxes. These taxes currently account for only a small fraction of total tax revenues in Kazakhstan. Distortions in property valuation and a weak connection to broader economic activities further reduce their effectiveness as fiscal tools for stimulating regional development. Box 1 explores scenarios involving a shift from cadastral to market-based property tax valuations.

The share of personal property tax in the local budget can vary significantly depending on the country, the region, and the structure of the local tax system. However, in most countries, personal property tax is one of the components of local income, as it is usually one of the taxes that go to local budgets and are used to finance local needs such as infrastructure improvements, education, health care, and other social services.

In Kazakhstan, for example, personal property tax is part of local taxes. Its share in local budgets may vary depending on a number of factors, including the level of income of the population, the degree of development of local economies, and the effectiveness of tax collection. In large cities and regional centers, the share of property taxes is higher than in rural areas owing to the sheer number of real estate properties and their higher cost.

Box 1

Property Tax: From Cadastral to Market-Based Valuations

Currently, property taxes in Kazakhstan are levied by subnational governments based on cadastral values, which are significantly lower than market values. Box Table B1.1 presents three scenarios where property taxes are applied to market values instead of cadastral values, while maintaining the same tax rate. The scenarios assume cadastral values are 50% (baseline), 30% (optimistic), or 70% (conservative) of market values.

Box Table B1.1: Property Tax Revenues under Optimistic, Baseline and Conservative Scenarios

Region	Current 2023 Revenues (T million)	Baseline Scenario (revenues in T million)	Optimistic Scenario (revenues in T million)	Conservative Scenario (revenues in T million)
Abay	11.077	22.155	36.924	15.825
Akmola	11.155	22.309	37.182	15.935
Aktobe	26.666	53.333	88.888	38.095
Almaty	15.257	30.514	50.856	21.796
Atyrau	83.532	167.065	278.441	119.332
West Kazakhstan	7.121	14.242	23.737	10.173
Zhambyl	14.411	28.821	48.035	20.586
Zhetisu	5.829	11.658	19.429	8.327
Karaganda	14.907	29.815	49.691	21.296
Kostanay	8.979	17.959	29.932	12.828
Kyzylorda	10.691	21.383	35.638	15.273
Mangystau	30.795	61.591	102.651	43.993
Pavlodar	16.949	33.899	56.498	24.213
North Kazakhstan	4.771	9.543	15.904	6.816
Turkestan	13.896	27.792	46.321	19.852
Ulytau	11.699	23.397	38.996	16.712
East Kazakhstan	8.424	16.847	28.079	12.034
Astana city	36.703	73.406	122.343	52.433
Almaty city	36.320	72.640	121.067	51.886
Shymkent city	12.798	25.597	42.661	18.283

Source: Authors' calculations based on data from the Bureau of National Statistics of the Agency for Strategic Planning and Reforms of the Republic of Kazakhstan.

continued on next page

Box 1 *continued*

Box Figure B1.1 presents the total amount of potential revenues under each scenario at the national level.

Box Figure B1.1: Potential National Revenues (T million) **Under Each Scenario**

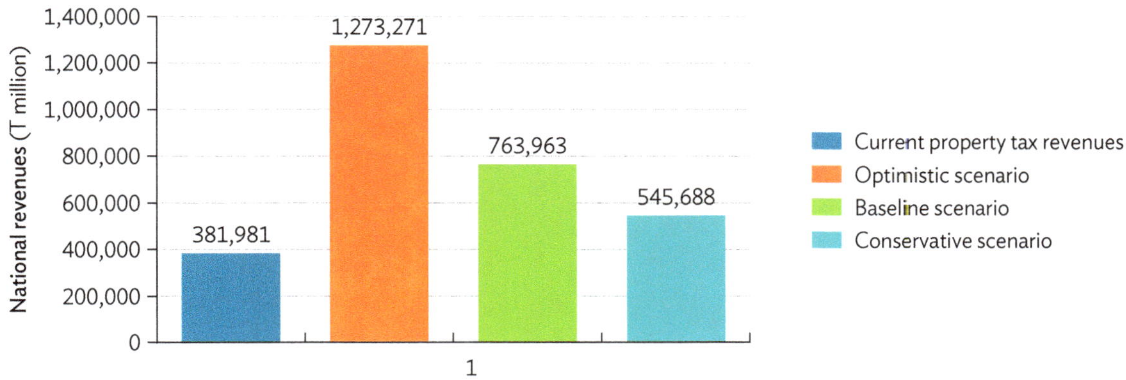

Source: Authors' calculations based on data from the Bureau of National Statistics of the Agency for Strategic Planning and Reforms of the Republic of Kazakhstan.

Transitioning to market-based property valuations could significantly increase local revenues. However, maintaining the same tax rate under such a shift may reduce compliance rates as taxpayers face significantly higher taxes. A more pragmatic approach would involve lowering the tax rate when transitioning to market values. Box Table B1.2 outlines revenue projections under the same three scenarios but assuming a tax rate reduced to 50% of the current rate.

Box Table B1.2: Property Tax Revenues under Optimistic, Baseline and Conservative Scenarios, and a Halved Tax Rate

Region	Current 2023 Revenues (T million)	Baseline Scenario (revenues in T million)	Optimistic Scenario (revenues in T million)	Conservative Scenario (revenues in T million)
Abay	11.077	11.077	18.462	7.912
Akmola	11.155	11.155	18.591	7.968
Aktobe	26.666	26.666	44.444	19.047
Almaty	15.257	15.257	25.428	10.898
Atyrau	83.532	83.532	139.220	59.666

table continued on next page

continued on next page

Box 1 *continued*

Box Table B1.2 *continued*

Region	Current 2023 Revenues (T million)	Baseline Scenario (revenues in T million)	Optimistic Scenario (revenues in T million)	Conservative Scenario (revenues in T million)
West Kazakhstan	7.121	7.121	11.868	5.086
Zhambyl	14.411	14.411	24.018	10.293
Zhetisu	5.829	5.829	9.715	4.163
Karaganda	14.907	14.907	24.846	10.648
Kostanay	8.979	8.979	14.966	6.414
Kyzylorda	10.691	10.691	17.819	7.637
Mangystau	30.795	30.795	51.325	21.997
Pavlodar	16.949	16.949	28.249	12.107
North Kazakhstan	4.771	4.771	7.952	3.408
Turkestan	13.896	13.896	23.160	9.926
Ulytau	11.699	11.699	19.498	8.356
East Kazakhstan	8.424	8.424	14.039	6.017
Astana city	36.703	36.703	61.171	26.216
Almaty city	36.320	36.320	60.533	25.943
Shymkent city	12.798	12.798	21.330	9.142

Source: Authors' calculations based on data from the Bureau of National Statistics of the Agency for Strategic Planning and Reforms of the Republic of Kazakhstan.

The adjusted baseline scenario approximates current revenues, while the optimistic scenario could nearly double them. The conservative scenario yields slightly lower revenues. The comparison across the scenarios is shown in Box Figure B1.2.

In Kazakhstan, the estimated value of real estate is considerably lower than its market value, which undermines the accuracy of property taxation. To address this discrepancy, it is recommended that a comprehensive inventory of the housing stock be conducted at the local level to ensure an up-to-date assessment of existing properties. Engaging professional appraisal companies can further enhance the real estate taxation process by providing more precise valuations and reassessing the estimated value of properties.

continued on next page

Box 1 *continued*

Additionally, implementing regular updates to real estate valuations or introducing an indexing mechanism would help maintain a more accurate reflection of property values over time. Considering the adoption of market or rental value as a more precise indicator of actual property worth could further improve the fairness and effectiveness of the taxation system.

Box Figure B1.2: Potential National Revenues (T million) **Under Each Scenario with 50% of Current Tax Rate**

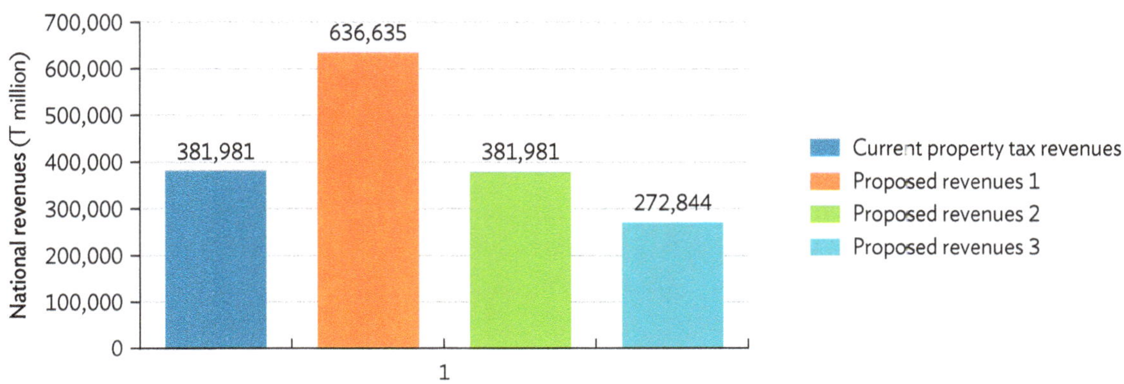

Source: Authors' elaboration based on data from the Bureau of National Statistics of the Agency for Strategic Planning and Reforms of the Republic of Kazakhstan.

Across the world, the property tax calculation procedure is standard in most cases, but there are differences in approaches to determining the tax base. In different countries, the market (Canada, Norway, Sweden, and the United States) or cadastral (Italy, Russia, and Spain) real estate values can be used, as can the cost of renting an object (Belgium and Luxembourg). In some countries, the tax is calculated depending on the total or usable area of housing using rates and adjustment coefficients set by government agencies. Various factors such as area, location, and type of building can also be taken into account to determine the tax base.

Property tax rates may be single at the national level or vary depending on the region. The approach by which rates are set by municipalities is more common in international practice. Differentiated rates can also be used, determined based on the value of the property.

A key aspect in calculating property taxes is the availability of an effective system for estimating the value of objects in the country, as well as the regularity of its revision. In different countries, the reassessment may be carried out at different intervals, for example annually or every 2 years. Carrying out a regular reassessment often requires significant financial costs. In this regard, there are cases when property value indexation can be applied instead of revaluation.

It should be borne in mind that in Kazakhstan the estimated value of facilities is significantly lower than the market value. In this regard, in order to accurately calculate the property tax, it is necessary:

- to carry out an inventory of the housing stock on site;
- to involve professional valuation companies to improve the process of taxation of real estate and review the estimated value of objects;
- to regularly update real estate valuations or apply a mechanism for indexing value;
- to consider using the market or rental value as a more accurate indicator of the actual value of the property.

Granting local governments the authority to adjust tax rates, grant exemptions, or implement tax holidays for development projects could optimize these revenues to address local needs. Such measures can improve the use of resources and mobilize local economic potential. However, property taxes alone are insufficient for achieving meaningful fiscal autonomy, underscoring the need for complementary measures.

Similarly, granting local governments in Kazakhstan greater autonomy in spending their resources could lead to significant improvements in public service delivery, economic efficiency, and regional development. Local officials, being closer to their communities, are better positioned to understand and respond to specific regional needs, whether in infrastructure, education, health care, or other essential services. This flexibility would allow for more targeted investments, reducing inefficiencies associated with centralized budget allocations that may not fully align with local priorities (World Bank 2021). Additionally, greater spending discretion could foster innovation in service delivery, as local governments experiment with policies tailored to their unique challenges. This, in turn, could enhance regional competitiveness, attract investment, and promote balanced economic growth across the country. Moreover, when local governments control more of their own spending, they become more accountable to their residents, strengthening public trust and incentivizing efficient use of resources (World Bank 2021). Ultimately, expenditure decentralization could help bridge regional disparities in Kazakhstan, ensuring all areas—urban and rural alike—benefit from more responsive and effective governance.

(b) Greater Freedom over Central Government Funding Streams

A more transformative approach to fiscal decentralization involves consolidating national funding into a flexible "single pot" for regional distribution. Currently, Kazakhstan's central government allocates funding for infrastructure, health care, and education through fragmented program-specific channels. By consolidating these streams into a unified pool, regional governments could allocate resources according to local priorities, reducing inefficiencies and enabling long-term planning.

Such a system would facilitate skills development, align infrastructure investment with industrial objectives, and address region-specific challenges. Empowering local authorities to allocate resources in alignment with their unique strategies could foster more cohesive regional development. However, while a single pot system represents a significant step forward, it does not constitute full fiscal devolution. True fiscal decentralization requires local governments to have independent authority to collect and manage their own taxes, free from central government oversight.

(c) Retaining a Share of National Taxes Locally

Worldwide, one of the most impactful approaches to fiscal decentralization involves allowing regions to retain a share of major national taxes, such as PIT, CIT, or VAT. Currently, VAT goes to the republican budget, and the PIT and part of the CIT—originating from SMEs—go to local budgets. Enabling regions to retain a portion of these revenues would provide them with a more stable and predictable funding source, reducing reliance on central transfers.

Retaining a larger share of CIT revenues at the local level would incentivize regions to attract high-paying jobs, boost employment, and support local businesses. This alignment of local economic strategies with revenue generation would create a virtuous cycle, wherein investments in industries and workforce development generate returns that can be reinvested locally. Box 2 illustrates a scenario for additional CIT and VAT devolution in Kazakhstan.

By retaining shares of national taxes such as CIT and VAT, regions would gain access to a more predictable revenue stream. This shift could empower local governments to drive economic development, address regional disparities, and contribute to a more balanced national growth trajectory.

Box 2

Greater Devolution of Corporate Income Tax and Value-Added Tax to Local Budgets: An Illustrative Scenario

Currently, approximately 23% of corporate income tax (CIT) collected across Kazakhstan is directly redistributed to local budgets. This 23% corresponds to CIT revenues from small and medium-sized enterprises (SMEs), while the remaining 77% remains in the national budget. We simulate a scenario where 50% of CIT—an increase of 27 percentage points—is retained by local budgets at the regional level (Box Figure B2.1).

In Box Figure B2.1, we can see the additional CIT revenues on top of the existing shares. These calculations use CIT revenues from SMEs as a reference point. While this may not capture the exact distribution of larger companies across Kazakhstani regions, it provides a relevant approximation of industrial agglomerations. Regions with significant industrial bases, such as Almaty city, Astana city, and Atyrau, would receive substantial funds under this scenario.

Similarly, value-added tax (VAT) revenues in Kazakhstan are currently retained at the national level. In other countries, including Germany, Russia, and South Africa, VAT revenues are redistributed to regional budgets through formulas, while in federal nations such as Brazil and Canada, regions or states retain part or all VAT revenues.

Box Figure B2.2 presents additional funds that would be transferred to Kazakhstani local budgets if 50% of VAT revenues were redistributed to regions based on population alone. Under this scenario, populous regions such as Almaty city and Turkestan would receive significant additional inflows, while less populous regions such as Ulytau, North Kazakhstan, and Abay would receive less than T100,000 million. In practice, in countries like Germany, more complex formulas are often employed to ensure equitable distribution. However, this scenario demonstrates the magnitude of additional resources that VAT redistribution could provide to local budgets.

continued on next page

Box 2 *continued*

Box Figure B2.1: Potential Additional Local Revenues (T million) **with 50% of Corporate Income Tax Retained Locally**

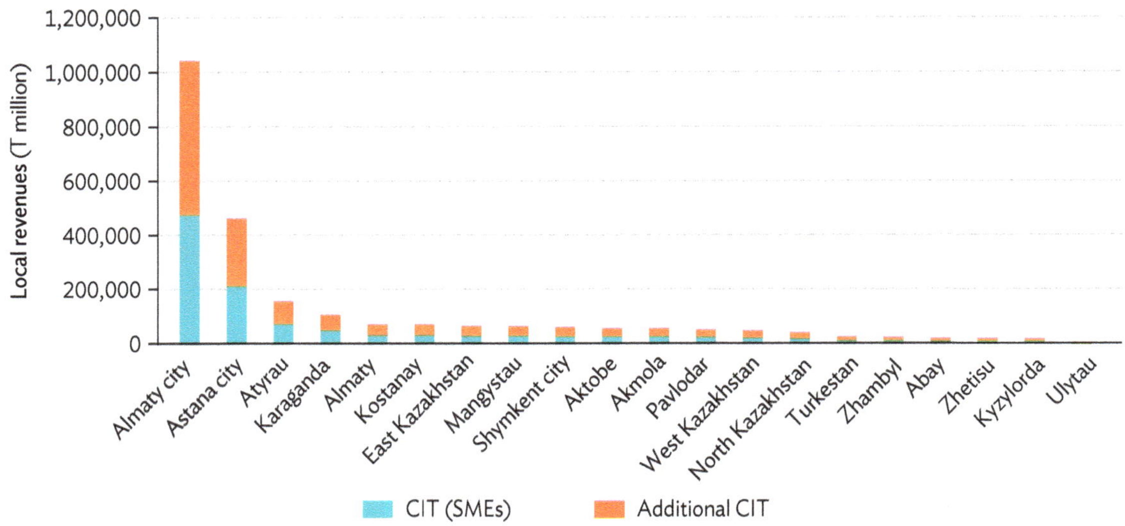

CIT = corporate income tax, SMEs = small and medium-sized enterprises.

Box Figure B2.2: Additional Funds from Value-Added (T million)

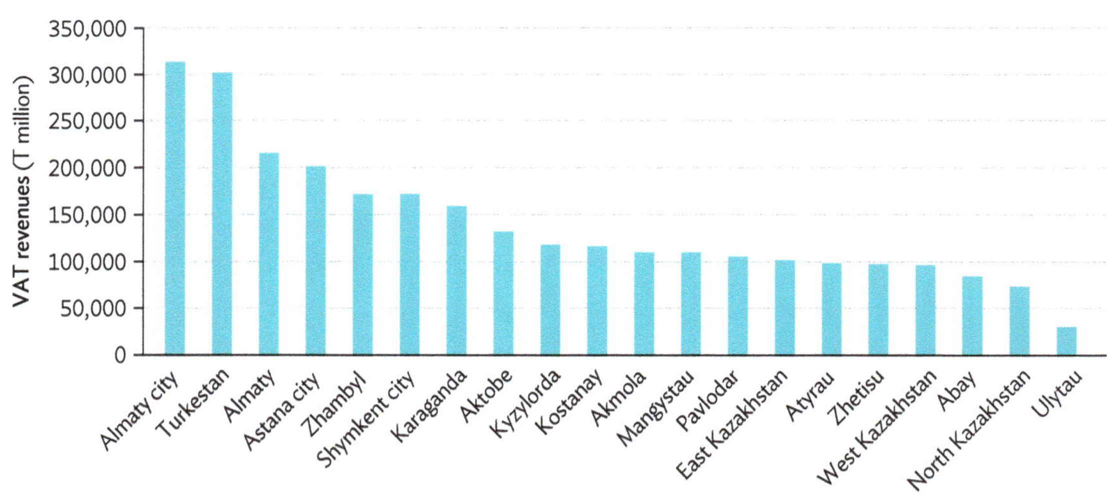

VAT = value-added tax.

Source: Authors' elaboration based on data from the Bureau of National Statistics of the Agency for Strategic Planning and Reforms of the Republic of Kazakhstan.

(d) Allowing Regions to Levy New Taxes or Charges

Empowering local governments to introduce new taxes—targeting areas such as tourism, environmental sustainability, or infrastructure—could provide tailored revenue streams to address local priorities. However, recent experiences in Kazakhstan highlight challenges with implementing such taxes. Earlier this year, the government canceled a recently introduced accommodation tax for foreign tourists, as it proved difficult to administer and incentivized shifts to alternative accommodations, such as apartments listed on local platforms like Airbnb. These accommodations were exempt from the tax, leading to an uneven playing field and increased lobbying from the hotel sector. Reintroducing such a tax risks further incentivizing the shadow economy, making its viability questionable.

Environmental fees, already charged for entry to national parks, offer another example. These fees are relatively low and have faced administrative challenges, limiting their effectiveness in funding sustainable development and conservation initiatives. Addressing these issues—through enhanced fee structures, improved administration, and targeted reinvestment—could help maximize the potential of such revenue streams while avoiding inefficiencies observed in the past.

While introducing new taxes may face political resistance, it offers an effective mechanism for regions to achieve financial independence and foster targeted development. When strategically aligned with regional industries, such taxes can promote sustainable economic growth that reflects local needs and priorities. To ensure broad public acceptance, these taxes should be designed to have minimal impact on local residents while providing essential funding to enhance services, infrastructure, and overall quality of life.

(e) Ability to Vary Rates of Existing Taxes

A more ambitious step in fiscal decentralization would involve granting regions the authority to adjust the rates of existing national taxes. This autonomy would enable regions to craft competitive tax policies tailored to attract businesses and residents, creating more favorable conditions for investment, economic growth, and the retention of a highly skilled workforce.

However, such autonomy carries the risk of initiating a "race to the bottom" in tax competition, where regions aggressively lower tax rates to attract investment, potentially eroding overall public revenues. This dynamic has been observed in countries like Brazil and the United States, where states have engaged in unsustainable tax competition.

To mitigate this risk, Kazakhstan could adopt a model similar to Germany's, where municipalities are allowed to adjust tax rates within specified limits. This controlled approach is reinforced by robust equalization mechanisms that maintain a resource balance across regions. Such a system ensures tax rate variations support regional competitiveness without undermining public service funding or exacerbating disparities.

By combining tax rate flexibility with equalization measures, Kazakhstan could empower local governments to attract investment and drive economic growth while safeguarding regional stability and equity. This model would allow regions to develop competitive tax environments that promote sustainable economic development and balanced national growth.

The Devolution Ladder

The five scenarios outlined represent incremental stages on what can be defined as a "devolution ladder." These stages range from minimal devolution to the fully decentralized model described in Scenario (e). Figure 15 provides a visual representation of these stages.

Figure 15: Fiscal Devolution Ladder

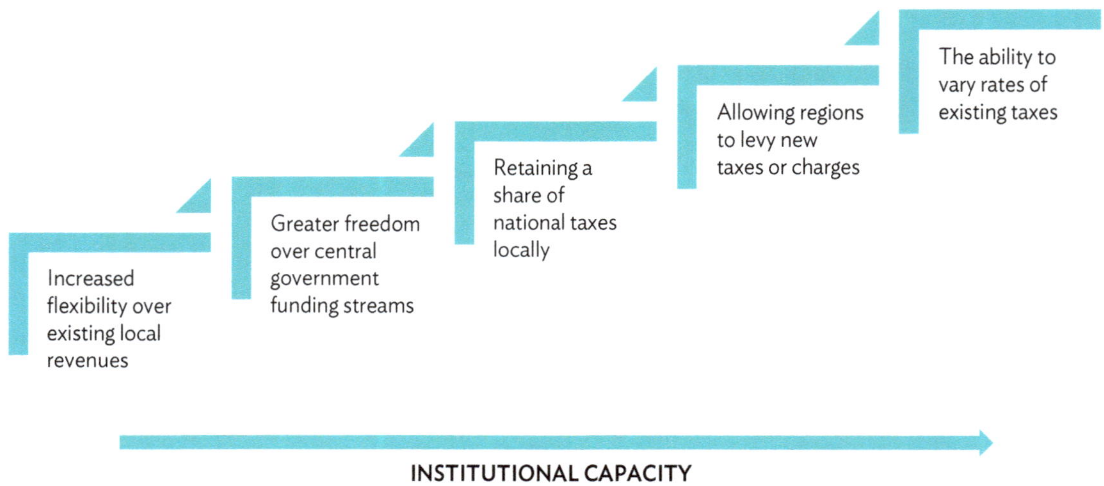

Source: Authors' elaboration.

For Kazakhstan, the most impactful approach to fiscal decentralization would involve combining several of the strategies discussed. Retaining a share of national taxes locally could give regions a direct stake in fostering economic growth, as they would benefit from increases in local economic activity. Additionally, granting local governments the authority to introduce new taxes and adjust existing tax rates within specified ranges would allow them to develop fiscal policies tailored to regional needs.

That said, it is important to note that the transfer of taxing powers from central to subnational governments often comes with certain conditions, or "strings," attached. These may include specific requirements on how the transferred funds can be used, such as mandates to allocate spending toward particular sectors like infrastructure, health care, or education. Additionally, performance-based conditions may be set, requiring local governments to meet certain fiscal or governance standards to qualify for or maintain these transfers. In some cases, local governments may need to raise matching funds or implement certain tax policies in alignment with central government priorities. These restrictions can limit the flexibility and autonomy of subnational governments, impacting their ability to tailor fiscal policies to local needs and priorities. Therefore, the effectiveness of fiscal transfers and tax incentives can be heavily influenced by the specific terms and conditions attached to these funds.

Effective fiscal decentralization in Kazakhstan, however, requires robust equalization mechanisms to address significant regional disparities. These mechanisms would ensure all regions can adequately fund essential services while fostering economic growth and development. Implementing these reforms would empower regions to design their own growth strategies, reduce reliance on central government transfers, and build a more balanced, resilient national economy that leverages local strengths and opportunities.

While fiscal decentralization can enhance regional and local growth, improve macroeconomic stability, and expand access to public services (Martínez-Vázquez, Lago-Peñas, and Sacchi 2017), it also presents challenges. Devolution of powers and resources is most effective when accompanied by strong local governance, accountability, and the capacity to manage public resources efficiently. Without these safeguards, decentralization risks exacerbating corruption and mismanagement of public funds.

Decentralization has a dual nature. On the one hand, it can reduce corruption by enhancing accountability, increasing competition among local governments, and providing greater transparency through additional "exit" and "voice" mechanisms at the subnational level (Ivanyna and Shah 2011; Altunbas and Thornton 2012). Evidence suggests fiscal decentralization has stronger positive effects on local economies in contexts of democratic governance, where elections and yardstick competition increase accountability (Martínez-Vázquez 2017). On the other hand, decentralization can weaken central monitoring, creating opportunities for corruption (Prud'homme 1995). Political decentralization may also increase risks of clientelism and capture by interest groups, particularly where powerful local elites dominate politics (Fan, Lin, and Treisman 2009).

Against this backdrop, Kazakhstan is already considering the conditions under which political decentralization could yield greater economic benefits for local and regional economies. At present, elections are held for the Parliament (the Majilis and the Senate) and the regional and city councils (*maslikhats*). In a 2024 address to the nation, President Tokayev announced a transition to direct elections for *akims* (governors/mayors) of districts and cities of regional significance from 2025 (Government of Kazakhstan 2024). Such a strengthening of democratic governance in local governments would enhance accountability, providing strong incentives for the efficient management of resources within a decentralized fiscal system.

Building the capacity of local governments is essential for effective decentralization. Training, digital tools, and financial oversight mechanisms are critical to achieving this objective. Increased responsibilities for tax collection at local and regional levels must be matched by sufficient administrative capacity.

Efforts to strengthen tax collection often emphasize knowledge-sharing and capacity-building initiatives integrated into national strategic plans. For example, the Italian Revenue Agency has incorporated tax administration capacity enhancement into its medium- and long-term taxation strategies. These include a public performance plan with clear management systems, objectives, and guidelines for effective implementation (OECD 2022). Similarly, the Canada Revenue Agency's Knowledge Sharing Platform is an online tool designed to promote best practices among tax administrations and regional tax organizations. It provides access to training from the OECD and other international bodies, highlighting successful approaches to tax collection (OECD 2022). Such initiatives are critical to equipping local and regional administrations to meet their tax revenue responsibilities.

Table 4 outlines eight actions and reforms essential for successfully implementing fiscal decentralization in Kazakhstan.

Table 4: Actions Needed for Successful Decentralization in Kazakhstan and International Examples

Actions Needed for Decentralization	International Example	Kazakhstan's Approach
Training and professional development programs	**South Africa:** Fiscal decentralization was supported by extensive training and development programs for local government officials. Through partnerships with institutions like the South African Local Government Association (SALGA), staff received training in budgeting, financial management, and transparent procurement processes.	Kazakhstan could develop similar training schemes focused on fiscal management, public finance, and administrative skills for regional and municipal officials. Partnering with local universities or international institutions would ensure high-quality, globally aligned training.
Strengthening local revenue generation and financial management skills	**Brazil:** Municipalities were supported by federal initiatives to enhance local revenue through improved property tax administration and business tax collection. The federal government provided training and resources to optimize tax assessments, collection processes, and financial management.	Kazakhstan could establish specialized training for subnational administrators in revenue collection and financial management, including workshops on property tax valuation, business tax administration, and effective budgeting techniques.
Building robust data collection and analytical capabilities	**Canada:** Local governments use advanced data collection and analytics to manage budgets and plan effectively. Many municipalities monitor economic, demographic, and social data to make evidence-based decisions and allocate resources efficiently.	Kazakhstan can improve subnational data capabilities by investing in digital tools and training. Equipping local governments with geographic information system technology, analytics software, and training on their use could strengthen evidence-based budgeting and planning.
Encouraging public–private partnerships (PPPs)	**India:** Subnational governments increasingly use PPPs to finance and manage infrastructure projects, especially in more developed states like Gujarat and Maharashtra. Local officials receive training on structuring contracts, negotiating agreements, and maintaining oversight, ensuring partnerships are sustainable and beneficial.	Kazakhstan could provide training to local officials on PPPs, enabling them to identify viable projects, negotiate contracts, and manage partnerships effectively.
Implementing performance-based accountability systems	**Philippines:** The Seal of Good Local Governance program rewards local governments that meet standards for transparency, fiscal management, and service delivery with additional funding and recognition.	Kazakhstan could establish a similar system to reward local administrations for strong fiscal management, transparency, and improved public services.

continued on next page

Table 4 *continued*

Actions Needed for Decentralization	International Example	Kazakhstan's Approach
Establishing intergovernmental coordination mechanisms	**Germany:** Germany's decentralized system includes coordination through regular conferences and decision-making forums between federal, state, and local governments. These structures facilitate best practice sharing, policy alignment, and collaborative problem solving.	Kazakhstan could create regular dialogue forums between regional and national officials for shared planning and coordination. Establishing intergovernmental councils would help align fiscal policies and support regional governments in managing new responsibilities.
Creating supportive legal and institutional frameworks	**Indonesia:** The 2001 decentralization reforms included a comprehensive legal framework defining subnational roles in financial management and governance, providing structure and clarity to decentralization efforts.	Kazakhstan could enhance its legal framework by clearly defining subnational roles in budgeting, tax collection, and accountability. This would reduce ambiguity, improve oversight, and support effective fiscal management.
Developing digital governance platforms	**Estonia:** Estonia's e-governance model integrates digital platforms for services like tax filing and permit applications, improving transparency and efficiency. These systems streamline local fiscal management and reduce bureaucratic delays.	Kazakhstan could adopt digital governance platforms for subnational administrations, facilitating online tax collection, reporting, and real-time budget monitoring. These systems would enhance transparency, efficiency, and communication between levels of government.

Source: Authors' elaboration based on Fitrani et al. (2005), Hegele and Behnke (2017), SALGA (2020), IIPA (2022), Porrúa et al. (2022), and IDB (2023).

Kazakhstan has the potential to empower regional governments to manage their expanded fiscal responsibilities effectively. Tailored training programs, enhanced revenue management systems, performance-based accountability measures, and advanced digital platforms are essential for successful fiscal decentralization. Drawing on international best practices, Kazakhstan can develop robust and capable subnational administrations, fostering sustainable and inclusive economic growth across the country.

Specific Recommendations on Taxes To Be Devolved to the Local Level

Fiscal decentralization, achieved through the redistribution of tax revenues, serves as a strategic mechanism to enhance regional financial independence and promote economic sustainability. As part of Kazakhstan's ongoing fiscal decentralization reforms, an evaluation has been conducted to identify potential tax revenue sources that could be reassigned to regional and municipal budgets, thereby reducing dependence on national transfers.

The evaluation of taxes to be devolved starts with considering the principles for "good tax devolution" (Institute for Government 2018). There is consensus in the literature that taxes whose burdens can be shifted beyond the expenditure benefit zone should not be devolved. Moreover, there should be a preference for taxes that can be administered at a reasonable cost and that are more "understandable" to the relevant constituencies.

This analysis focuses exclusively on tax revenues currently allocated to the republican budget, excluding those of national significance, such as customs duties on exported goods and special anti-dumping and countervailing duties regulated under the Treaty on the Eurasian Economic Union. Consideration has also been given to the contributions of individual regions to the republican budget to ensure an equitable distribution of tax resources. For example, excise tax revenues from domestically produced tobacco products are presently allocated solely to Almaty region, where production is concentrated, limiting the ability of other regions to generate revenue from this source. Additionally, a comprehensive review of the legislative framework has identified territorial restrictions, such as those governing gambling taxes, which are levied only in Almaty and Akmola owing to national regulations prohibiting gambling elsewhere in Kazakhstan.

Following this assessment, two tax revenue sources have been identified for potential transfer from the republican budget to regional and municipal budgets: the fee for the use of the radio frequency spectrum and the fee for digital mining. In 2023, revenues from the radio frequency spectrum fee amounted to T165.1 billion, representing 1.3% of total tax revenues to the republican budget. The majority of this revenue was generated in Almaty (T161.5 billion) and Astana (T3.1 billion), while significantly smaller amounts were recorded in Zhetisu region (T2.4 million). Similarly, tax revenues from digital mining fees totaled T5.0 billion, accounting for 0.04% of total tax revenues. Astana contributed the largest share (T4.0 billion), while Abay and Akmola regions recorded minimal contributions of T304,000 and T359,000, respectively. Table 5 presents a breakdown of these revenues by region.

Table 5: Revenues from the Two Proposed Taxes

Regions, Cities of Republican Significance, the Capital	Fee for Use of Radio Frequency Spectrum (T'000)	Fee for Digital Mining (T'000)
Kazakhstan	165,113,112	4,967,506
Abay region	9,696	304
Akmola region	41,249	359
Aktobe region	33,371	212,079
Almaty region	4,647	3,429
Atyrau region	55,609	15,655
West Kazakhstan region	16,721	–89,265
Zhambyl region	7,682	118,068
Zhetisu region	2,409	16,030
Karaganda region	37,591	274,929

continued on next page

Table 5 *continued*

Regions, Cities of Republican Significance, the Capital	Fee for Use of Radio Frequency Spectrum (T'000)	Fee for Digital Mining (T'000)
Kostanay region	29,971	1,082
Kyzylorda region	26,899	0
Mangystau region	66,633	–11
Pavlodar region	53,572	340,799
North Kazakhstan region	25,262	0
Turkestan region	5,803	0
Ulytau region	13,224	0
East Kazakhstan region	25,518	–40,665
Astana	3,081,767	4,013,068
Almaty	161,548,277	101,644
Shymkent	27,212	0

Source: Authors' elaboration based on Ministry of Finance of the Republic of Kazakhstan data.

The transfer of tax revenues from fees for the use of the radio frequency spectrum and digital mining fees from the republican budget to local budgets has the potential to contribute to the financial independence of regional governments. This reallocation could, in turn, reduce reliance on transfers from the central government, leading to greater fiscal self-sufficiency at the local level.

In 2023, the contribution of these fees to the total grants received from the national budget varied significantly across regions. The highest share was recorded in Pavlodar, where these revenues accounted for 0.3% of total grants, amounting to T394.4 million. In contrast, Turkestan region recorded the lowest share, with only 0.001% of its grants derived from these sources, equivalent to T5.8 million. Figure 16 summarizes the additional contributions by region.

Overall, the total revenues from these fees contributed 3.4% to the aggregate amount of grants transferred from the republican budget to local budgets. This redistribution mechanism highlights the potential for strengthening regional financial autonomy by ensuring a more equitable allocation of tax revenues across Kazakhstan's administrative divisions.

Three possible scenarios for fiscal decentralization have been identified, each based on the transfer of specific tax revenue sources to local budgets. These scenarios consider the economic characteristics of different regions and the potential for stimulating investment, infrastructure development, and technological innovation.

Figure 16: Regional Contributions of the Devolution of Radio Frequency and Digital Mining Taxes to the Local Level

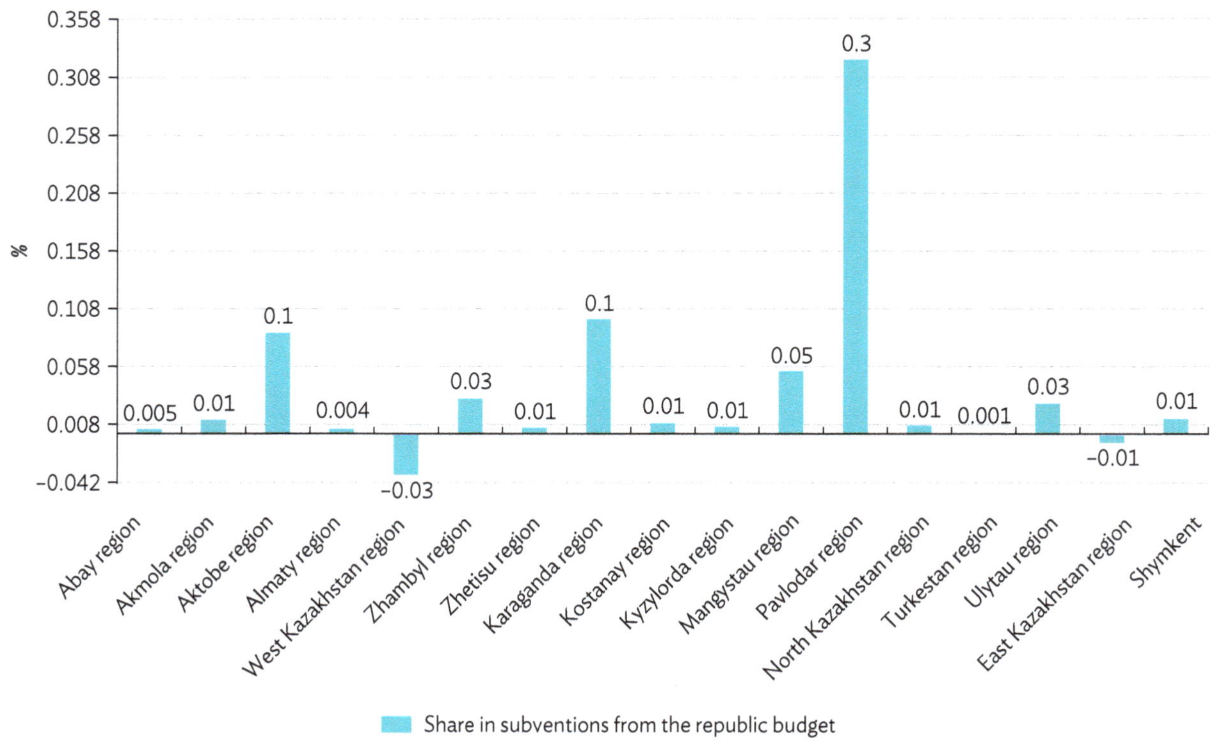

Source: Authors' elaboration based on Ministry of Finance of the Republic of Kazakhstan data.

Scenario 1: Decentralization of Revenue from the Radio Frequency Spectrum Fee

The first scenario involves transferring revenue from fees for the use of the radio frequency spectrum from the national level to local budgets, granting local authorities the power to regulate and, if necessary, adjust fee rates. This adjustment would be based on regional economic conditions, including the need to develop telecommunications infrastructure, attract investment, and support innovative technologies. Additionally, local authorities would have the option to introduce tax incentives to stimulate economic activity in the sector. In 2023, revenue from these fees accounted for 2.3% of subventions from the republican budget and 3.3% of total transfers.

Fiscal decentralization in this context presents significant opportunities for enhancing digital infrastructure and spurring regional economic growth. By increasing fee rates, strengthening control over illegal spectrum use, and encouraging infrastructure investments, local governments could improve communication quality, generate additional tax revenue, and create new employment opportunities. Furthermore, supporting the adoption of advanced technologies such as 5G, streamlining permit procedures for infrastructure development, and attracting investments through tax incentives will contribute to the sector's long-term sustainability.

However, a balanced approach is required to avoid market overload, infrastructure strain, and potential negative impacts on competition and service accessibility. If implemented comprehensively, these measures could enhance the economic attractiveness of Kazakhstan's regions, accelerate digital transformation, and establish a robust telecommunications infrastructure capable of supporting sustainable development. Appendix 5 provides key indicators of the radio frequency spectrum in Kazakhstan.

Scenario 2: Decentralization of Revenue from the Digital Mining Fee

This scenario focuses on transferring revenue from fees for digital mining to local budgets, allowing local authorities to regulate and adjust fee rates.[4] This regulatory framework would account for regional economic conditions, particularly the need to develop energy infrastructure, attract investment, and support technological innovation. Local governments would also have the flexibility to introduce tax incentives aimed at promoting economic activity in the sector. In 2023, revenue from digital mining fees accounted for 0.1% of subventions from the republican budget and 0.07% of total transfers.

Decentralizing tax revenues from digital mining would create new financial opportunities for developing critical energy infrastructure projects. The expansion of renewable energy sources and modernization of the energy grid could generate additional revenue streams for local governments, while investments in these areas would require a skilled workforce, thereby reducing unemployment and improving social conditions.

Furthermore, an upgraded energy infrastructure would facilitate business activity and encourage production expansion, ultimately leading to higher tax revenues. By supporting the transition to renewable energy and increasing the efficiency of the electricity grid, local governments would not only strengthen the energy sector but also contribute to Kazakhstan's broader environmental and economic objectives. Appendix 6 outlines the primary indicators of digital mining in Kazakhstan.

Scenario 3: Combined Decentralization of the Radio Frequency Spectrum Fee and the Digital Mining Fee

The third scenario entails the transfer of revenue from both the radio frequency spectrum fee and the digital mining fee to local budgets, granting local authorities the power to regulate and adjust fee rates according to regional economic conditions. This approach would consider the need to develop energy and telecommunications infrastructure, attract investments, and foster technological innovation. Additionally, it would allow for the introduction of targeted tax incentives to stimulate economic activity in both sectors. In 2023, the combined revenue from these fees accounted for 2.4% of subventions from the republican budget and 3.4% of total transfers.

Implementing this scenario would provide greater financial autonomy to local governments, enabling them to design economic policies tailored to regional priorities. By decentralizing these revenue sources, regions would be better positioned to make targeted investments in infrastructure, driving long-term economic stability and sustainable regional development.

[4] Fiscal decentralization scenarios have been developed on the basis of the draft new Budget Code posted on the website of the Majilis of the Parliament of the Republic of Kazakhstan dated 28 September: https://mazhilis.parlam.kz/#/all-bill/pending-majilis.

On 15 March 2025, the new Budget Code of the Republic of Kazakhstan was adopted, according to which revenues from digital mining fees were transferred to local budgets (budgets of cities of republican significance, the capital, and regions).

Additional Local Tax Reforms for Tax Devolution

In addition to the taxes proposed, other local tax reforms can contribute to fostering local revenue generation, including enacting a property transfer tax, allowing for more local discretion for PIT rates in urban areas, and implementing local excise taxes (Bird and Vaillancourt 1998). As discussed, a shift to a market value-based property tax could enhance fairness and boost revenue, but it requires an updated valuation system and could face taxpayer resistance (Kitchen 2012). Introducing a piggyback PIT in urban areas with some local discretion would provide municipalities with an independent revenue stream and improve accountability. However, it could create regional tax disparities and would require strong administrative oversight. Similarly, a property transfer tax could be an effective way to capture revenue from high-value real estate transactions, but its volatility and potential negative impact on market liquidity must be carefully managed (López-Laborda and Onrubia 2005).

Other revenue-enhancing measures include business licenses, local excise taxes, and benefit taxes. Business licenses can generate stable revenues and promote compliance but should be structured to avoid overburdening small businesses. Local excise taxes, such as those on fuel or tobacco, can be an efficient revenue source if designed to prevent tax burden exportation to other regions (Bollinger and Sexton 2023). Additionally, benefit taxes and user charges, such as those on telecom services and refuse collection, ensure taxpayers contribute directly to the services they use, fostering financial sustainability. However, such charges must be carefully managed to avoid regressive impacts on lower-income households (World Bank 2021). Implementing these reforms in a balanced manner would enhance Kazakhstan's fiscal decentralization efforts while ensuring equitable and efficient service delivery across regions. Table 6 summarizes the main advantages and disadvantages of this set of additional tax reforms.

Finally, asymmetric tax devolution refers to a system in which different regions or municipalities within a country are granted varying degrees of taxing authority based on their economic capacity, administrative capability, or specific policy needs. This approach recognizes that some regions may have stronger tax bases and greater fiscal management capacity than others, allowing for a more tailored approach to fiscal decentralization (Allain-Dupre, Chatry, and Moisio 2020). In Kazakhstan, implementing asymmetric tax devolution could enable resource-rich regions, such as those with significant oil and gas revenues, to exercise more control over local taxation while providing additional central government support to less economically developed areas.

The potential benefits of asymmetric tax devolution in Kazakhstan include enhanced fiscal autonomy for high-revenue regions, allowing them to invest in infrastructure and public services without excessive central government oversight. This could lead to more efficient and responsive local governance. However, the approach also presents challenges, such as the risk of widening regional inequalities if wealthier regions retain a disproportionate share of revenues while poorer regions remain dependent on central transfers. To mitigate these disparities, Kazakhstan would need a robust equalization mechanism to ensure all regions, regardless of their economic strength, have adequate resources to provide essential public services. A well-balanced asymmetric tax devolution model could enhance local government efficiency while maintaining national fiscal cohesion.

Table 6: Advantages and Disadvantages of Additional Local Tax Reforms

Tax Reform	Pros	Cons
Shift to market value basis for property tax	□ Improves fairness by aligning tax with actual property values □ Increases local revenue, especially in growing urban areas □ Encourages efficient land use	□ Requires costly and complex valuation updates □ May cause taxpayer resistance owing to higher tax burdens □ Could disproportionately impact lower-income households without exemptions
Additional personal income tax rate discretion in urban areas	□ Provides independent revenue for local governments □ Enhances fiscal responsibility and accountability □ Can generate substantial revenue in high-income areas	□ Creates regional tax disparities, potentially affecting regional mobility □ Requires strong administrative capacity to manage variation □ Politically sensitive, as personal income tax increases are often unpopular
Enacting of a property transfer tax	□ Generates revenue from high-value property transactions □ Progressive tax targeting wealthier individuals □ Easy to administer compared to annual property taxes	□ May discourage property transactions and reduce market liquidity □ Revenue can be volatile, depending on transaction levels □ Risk of tax avoidance through underreporting prices
Business licenses as a revenue source	□ Stable and predictable revenue for local governments □ Ensure businesses contribute to local services □ Can promote market fairness and compliance	□ High fees may discourage small business growth □ Require strong enforcement to prevent tax evasion □ Can be seen as a burden for start-ups and small and medium-sized enterprises
Implementation of local excise taxes	□ Generates revenue with relatively low administrative costs □ Ensures local benefit from goods consumed within jurisdiction □ Can support public health or environmental goals	□ Must avoid tax burden being shifted to other regions (exported) □ May encourage cross-border shopping if rates differ □ Can disproportionately impact lower-income consumers
Benefit taxes and user charges (e.g., telecoms, refuse collection, services)	□ Ensure users contribute to the cost of services □ Encourage efficient service delivery and cost recovery □ Reduce reliance on broad-based taxation	□ Require strong billing and enforcement mechanisms □ Can be regressive, impacting low-income households more □ Public resistance may arise if charges are perceived as excessive

Source: Authors' elaboration based on Bird and Vaillancourt (1998), López-Laborda and Onrubia (2005), Kitchen (2012), World Bank (2021), and Bollinger and Sexton (2023).

FISCAL EQUALIZATION MECHANISMS

6

Importance of Fiscal Equalization

Fiscal redistribution has long been a cornerstone of public resource management. Over time, many countries have embedded the principles of fiscal redistribution and equalization into their governance frameworks. Today, nearly all developed nations and an increasing number of developing ones employ fiscal transfers to support less-developed municipalities and regions. These mechanisms are often grounded in equity concerns, addressing significant and persistent regional disparities observed across countries.

Metrics such as the Gini index and advanced tools like the Regional Development Trap Index have highlighted the depth of regional inequalities in regions across Europe, Latin America, and Asia (Iammarino, Rodriguez-Pose, and Storper 2019). These disparities are not only substantial but also have often proven enduring. Evidence suggests regional inequalities have intensified over the past decade in many nations (Rodriguez-Pose 2018).

In theory, fiscal redistribution seeks to promote equity by addressing disparities in fiscal capacity and the costs of providing public goods. These costs vary significantly between regions, driven by factors such as geographic location, population size, demographics, and growth trajectories (Rodriguez-Pose and Ezcurra 2010; Dougherty and Forman 2021). Redistribution mechanisms typically target either fiscal capacity or cost equalization to achieve their objectives.

Empirical evidence underscores the effectiveness of fiscal redistribution in reducing regional disparities. Studies show that monetary transfers through fiscal equalization significantly narrow gaps in fiscal capacity among regions. For example, fiscal equalization mechanisms have been shown to reduce disparities in fiscal capacity, as measured by the coefficient of variation, by nearly two-thirds, from 29% to 10% (Blöchlinger et al. 2007). Additionally, fiscal redistribution modestly reduces income inequality, as evidenced by decreases in the Gini coefficient. These results are consistent across both federal and unitary states (Blöchlinger et al. 2007).

Fiscal equalization remains a critical tool for achieving balanced development and equity across regions. By addressing fiscal imbalances, it ensures that less-developed areas have the resources necessary to provide public goods and services, thereby promoting greater socioeconomic cohesion. Further studies have confirmed that fiscal redistribution lowers interregional inequalities in per capita revenues (Dougherty and Forman 2021). But achieving the right form of fiscal equalization requires achieving a fine balance between economic, social, and political needs. Across the world, there are numerous examples of successful fiscal equalization systems. In particular, the experiences of Australia, Canada, and Germany provide valuable insights into the design and implementation of effective fiscal equalization systems (Appendix 2).

Australia's system, administered by the independent Commonwealth Grants Commission (CGC), ensures all states and territories can deliver comparable public services regardless of revenue disparities. Through a rigorous assessment of fiscal capacities and expenditure needs, as well as flexible and regular adjustments, the system allocates goods and services tax revenues equitably. By addressing economic imbalances while maintaining transparency and trust, the CGC has helped weaker states such as Tasmania and the Northern Territory invest in critical infrastructure, health care, and education, fostering long-term economic resilience.

Canada's equalization program offers a distinct model, balancing flexibility and stability, particularly for resource-dependent provinces. Its constitutional foundation and dynamic formula, which adjusts for natural resource revenues and economic fluctuations, ensure even vulnerable provinces can maintain essential public services.

Germany's *Finanzausgleich* system also stands out for its multilayered approach to reducing fiscal disparities among *Länder*. Combining vertical and horizontal transfers with supplementary federal grants, it ensures even economically weaker regions can provide equitable public services. Grounded in Germany's Basic Law, the system is characterized by transparency, predictability, and regular adjustments, enabling sustained investment in infrastructure and social services.

While all three systems have faced challenges, including regional tensions and political complexities, they illustrate the importance of robust frameworks, transparent administration, and adaptability in achieving fiscal equity and promoting national cohesion. Appendix 2 presents more on these systems.

Kazakhstan's Need for Fiscal Equalization

A recurring concern about fiscal decentralization in Kazakhstan is that unequal starting points among its oblasts could hinder the success of devolving tax powers. Kazakhstan's regional disparities are stark, with local economies exhibiting significant variation in their revenue bases and capacity to generate income. Figure 17 shows the variation in the share of PIT as a proportion of total tax revenues across the country's districts. For example, in districts such as Pavlodar and West Kazakhstan, PIT accounts for more than 40% of total tax revenues, while in other districts, including those in Akmola and Mangystau oblasts, it constitutes less than 15%. This disparity has raised concerns that increasing fiscal autonomy could exacerbate inequalities in a country where the vertical share (i.e., how total government revenue is divided between the national and subnational levels) is determined by national legislation and documented in Kazakhstan's Budget Code.[5] This would allow wealthier regions to prosper while less affluent areas remain resource constrained.

While these concerns are valid, they overlook how fiscal decentralization can be designed to address such disparities. Fiscal autonomy need not be a zero-sum game. Properly crafted equalization measures can balance greater fiscal freedom with national mechanisms that consider differences in regional revenue capacity and spending needs.

5 Appendix 4 of this report outlines the official distribution proportions for various taxes and fees among the tiers of the budget system.

Figure 17: Share of Personal Income Tax in Total Tax Revenues, by District, 2023

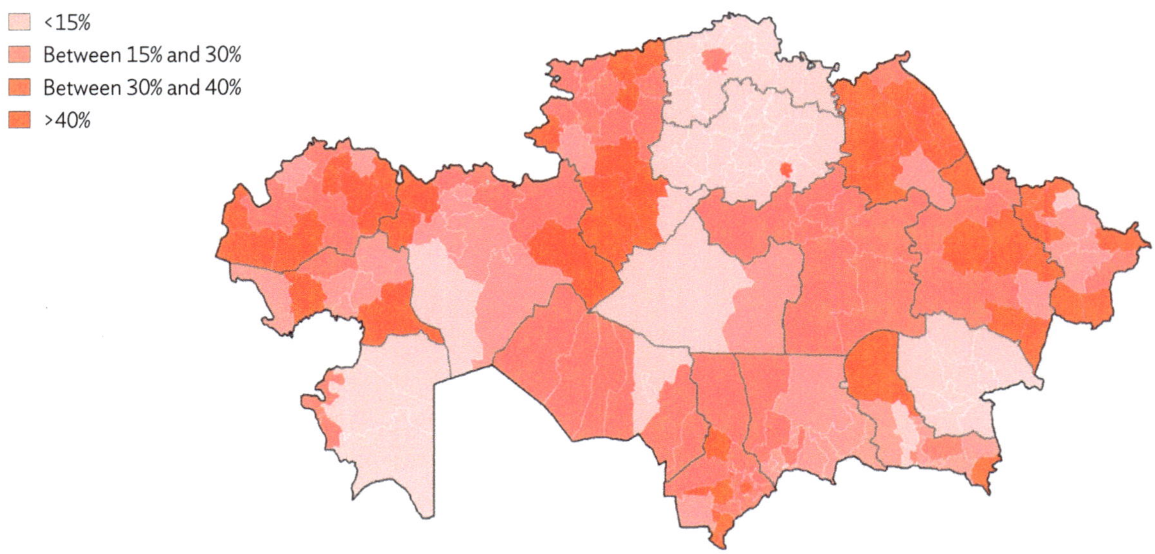

Source: Authors' elaboration based on data from the Bureau of National Statistics of the Agency for Strategic Planning and Reforms of the Republic of Kazakhstan

Denmark offers a pertinent example: its municipalities generate 70% of their revenue from local taxes, primarily PIT, supplemented by annual reviews of municipal revenue and expenditure needs. Equalization grants are then allocated to areas with structural revenue deficits, enabling Denmark to maintain regional disparities below the OECD median (OECD 2023b).

Frequent equalization reviews are critical for ensuring fiscal transfers reflect changes in each region's revenue-generating potential over time. Fiscal decentralization should foster incentives for local economic growth by aligning resources with regional development strategies. A formula-based equalization approach that accounts for both revenue capacity and spending needs could address Kazakhstan's uneven starting points while enabling regions to build sustainable revenue bases.

Kazakhstan's fiscal policies must balance immediate risks, such as economic slowdowns, with the long-term goal of promoting regional convergence and sustainability. Despite the country's highly centralized public finance system, regional inequalities persist, demonstrating that the current system of equalizing transfers has been insufficient to foster regional productivity and growth. This underscores the need for complementary measures. While some decentralization options may prove less effective, Kazakhstan should pursue strategies capable of driving regional economic development and reducing disparities.

Conditional transfers are one such measure that could equalize economic development across Kazakhstan's oblasts. These transfers target underperforming areas, focusing on priorities such as infrastructure and public services. Table 7 charts the types of conditional grants that could be implemented as part of vertical transfers from the central government to regions. These grants address high-priority areas crucial for regional development.

Table 7: Different Types of Conditional Grants and Their Benefits and Disadvantages

Type of Conditional Grant	Objectives	Desired Incentives	Undesired Incentives	Commonality
Earmarked nonmatching grants	◻ Provide financial resources for specific purposes without requiring matching funds ◻ Support regions with limited fiscal capacities ◻ Align with broader central government objectives	◻ Ensure funds are directed toward high-priority areas ◻ Enable regions with limited resources to undertake projects ◻ Reduce the financial burden on fiscally weak regions	◻ May distort local priorities if conditions are too stringent or misaligned ◻ Can be seen as central government overreach, limiting local autonomy	**Less common** (e.g., United Kingdom Pupil Premium, Canada Cultural Spaces Fund)
Earmarked matching open-ended grants	◻ Subsidize services with spillover benefits ◻ Encourage subnational governments to invest in specific areas ◻ Align with broader central government objectives	◻ Stimulate greater scrutiny and local ownership of projects ◻ Promote shared responsibility between different levels of government	◻ Matching requirements may deter poorer regions, exacerbating disparities ◻ Risk of inefficiency or misallocation due to substitution effects	**Common** (e.g., United States Medicaid, United Kingdom Affordable Homes Programme)
Earmarked matching close-ended grants	◻ Subsidize services with capped matching fund ◻ Encourage subnational governments to invest in specific areas ◻ Align with broader central government objectives	◻ Increase accountability and enhance cost transparency ◻ Enable better budget control for grantors ◻ Promote shared responsibility between government levels	◻ Matching requirements might deter poorer regions ◻ Risk of overspending in targeted areas, neglecting other sectors	**Less common** (e.g., France state-region planning contracts, Australia Roads to Recovery Program)
Performance-oriented transfers	◻ Reward subnational governments that achieve specific benchmarks ◻ Emphasize results and outcomes. Input flexibility is paramount ◻ Contractual platform with prespecified targets	◻ Promote efficiency, effectiveness, transparency, and accountability in service delivery ◻ Ensure funds are used for intended purposes	◻ Conditions must be attached to outputs, as opposed to outcomes, which are subject to interferences beyond the control of policymakers ◻ Limited by data availability ◻ Potential for data manipulation	**Less common** (e.g., United States Race to the Top Grant, Australia National Health Reform Agreement)

Source: Authors' elaboration based on OECD (2024a).

Matching grants, in particular, require subnational governments to cofinance projects with central funds, fostering greater local accountability and ownership of development initiatives (OECD 2024a).

Performance-based grants are gaining traction as a mechanism for conditional transfers. Also known as output-based grants, they link funding to specific outcomes, pushing subnational governments to align with national objectives and improve governance. Inspired by principles of new public management and institutional economics, they promote accountability and transparency by focusing on results rather than inputs.

Such grant systems typically involve annual assessments of subnational governments' performance. Funding adjustments reward high-performing regions or penalize underperformers, fostering a results-oriented approach. Performance-based grants may address overall governance, financial management, and transparency, or focus on sector-specific outcomes such as health care improvements. For instance, countries such as Argentina, Brazil, and India use sector-specific grants for health care, while ecological transfers in Brazil, France, and Portugal link fiscal incentives to environmental conservation efforts (Steffensen 2010; Shotton and Gankhuyag 2021).

Kazakhstan could benefit from adopting similar models. These mechanisms not only address existing inequalities but also establish a framework for sustainable growth, ensuring all regions have the resources and incentives to thrive within a fiscally decentralized system. By integrating conditional and performance-based grants into its equalization framework, Kazakhstan can achieve the flexibility and accountability necessary to mitigate disparities and support regional economic development effectively.

Finally, a few words about the territorial dimension for fiscal equalization. In Kazakhstan, the term "region" in this report refers primarily to oblasts (or the three cities with oblast status). Under the current Budget Code, central government transfers—commonly known as subventions or equalization grants—are directed to oblast budgets. Subsequently, oblast authorities may distribute a portion of those funds to lower tiers of government, which include raions (districts) and local municipalities (cities, towns, villages). However, many aspects of the existing arrangements can be criticized for weak transparency and for failing to reflect evolving socioeconomic conditions across smaller jurisdictions.

The decentralization recommendations in this report are directed primarily at expanding oblast-level revenue autonomy and strengthening oblast capacity to use these resources effectively. Nonetheless, some proposals—such as the possibility of devolving new local taxes or developing an asymmetric arrangement—could feasibly extend to the raion and municipal levels, particularly if these lower-tier governments demonstrate sufficient administrative capacity. The same principles of accountability and alignment of expenditure responsibilities would apply: transferring authority to those entities best placed to respond to local needs, provided they can manage revenue collection transparently and efficiently.

FISCAL EQUALIZATION SCENARIOS

7

Greater fiscal devolution to subnational levels requires robust equalization systems that are simple, predictable, and effective in redistributing transfers across regions. This section presents 10 scenarios incorporating various combinations of demographic, geographical, and socioeconomic variables. The methodology follows approaches used in countries such as Australia, Canada, and the PRC (Ma 1997; Shah 2007). These scenarios focus primarily on the equalization of expenditure needs, a methodology commonly employed in systems like Australia's. More complex systems, such as those based on equalization of fiscal capacity (as in Canada), are also effective but are typically used in federal systems where subnational governments have substantial tax autonomy—conditions that do not yet exist in Kazakhstan.

Challenges in Kazakhstan's Fiscal Equalization Formula

Kazakhstan's current fiscal equalization formula for calculating General Transfers is definitely complex. It includes a total of more than 200 data points to determine the transfer amount for each region. The formula is structured around the difference between projected revenue and projected expenditure, with some of data points used for revenue estimation and others for expenditure. The existing approach is based on historical data, which, on the one hand, ensures continuity but, on the other hand, may limit the flexibility of the system and its ability to adapt to new challenges. This helps maintain the established development trajectories and may reduce the incentives for structural changes in the field of regional fiscal management. In addition, the formula basis of the distribution does not always fully reflect the current economic realities and the specifics of the socioeconomic situation of various regions. As a result, the observed leveling effect remains subdued, and the potential for increasing fiscal sustainability in less well-off regions is not fully realized.

In addition, excessive reliance on past data in fiscal allocations is widely regarded as ineffective, as it can perpetuate inefficiencies and fail to account for changing economic conditions (Shah 2006). International experience suggests such a complex and resource-intensive approach often becomes unused and ineffective, and frequently leads to a misallocation of resources. For example, studies on fiscal equalization in Canada and Germany have demonstrated that basing transfers on historical spending patterns can discourage local governments from pursuing reforms or improving efficiency, as their future funding remains dependent on maintaining past expenditure levels (Baretti, Huber, and Lichtblau 2002).

Beyond recognizing the current system's reliance on a complex formula and historical budget data, further considerations exist that are essential to designing a new approach that will more effectively reduce regional inequalities:

(a) **Potential opportunity analysis:** The analysis of existing problems in the system of inter-budgetary equalization, along with the study of potential opportunities, can generate valuable lessons for future reforms. This will allow for a deeper understanding of both the directions of possible changes and the limitations that the process of modernizing the current system of inter-budgetary distribution may face.

(b) **Data management and quality:** Improved data management is critical to developing an equalization formula that aligns with national objectives. Key questions relate to the currency and accuracy of population statistics—particularly if these are updated only during census periods—and whether fiscal data are systematically audited and readily accessible. If there are concerns regarding the timeliness of budget records or demographic estimates, recalculating transfers using a more dynamic formula may fail to capture current conditions. Adequately resourcing and standardizing data collection processes would help ensure the equalization system is underpinned by reliable, annually updated indicators.

(c) **Clarity of objectives and the role of an independent commission:** Revisiting and restating the objectives of the grant system on a regular basis can help maintain focus on the core principles of equity and efficiency. In many countries, an independent grants commission—often staffed by technical experts—plays a significant role in reviewing allocation criteria and recommending formula modifications. The feasibility of introducing such a body in Kazakhstan hinges on political willingness to accept independent oversight and on the country's existing institutional capacity. If this model is adopted, the commission's recommendations would need to be seen as credible, transparent, and aligned with national development plans to gain acceptance among policymakers and subnational authorities.

(d) **Monitoring and evaluation:** Finally, robust monitoring and evaluation mechanisms should be established to measure the actual impact of each year's allocations on regional development outcomes. At present, understanding to what extent government agencies systematically monitor results or track whether transfers translate into tangible improvements in public services will depend on the effectiveness of fiscal alignment. A dedicated fiscal analysis unit—equipped to undertake periodic reviews of how funds are spent and what outcomes are achieved—can inform ongoing adjustments to the formula. Without regular evaluations, even well-crafted reforms risk either overshooting or undershooting the needs of beneficiary regions.

By grappling with these practical considerations, Kazakhstan can more adequately tackle the technical and political challenges of redesigning its equalization system.

Building Alternative Fiscal Equalization Scenarios

Addressing these weaknesses will entail shifting from formulas rooted in retrospective expenditure patterns to a more forward-looking, policy-driven model. The selection and weighting of variables—whether population, poverty levels, wellbeing indices, or development trap indicators—should mirror national goals of balancing growth with equity. While this recalibration of formulas requires addressing the difficulty of assigning appropriate weights and potential trade-offs, it is a necessary step if equalization is to bolster the broader objective of a more integrated and inclusive Kazakhstan. To ensure fiscal transfers in Kazakhstan promote equitable development and incentivize regional innovation, it would be advisable to incorporate more dynamic indicators, such as real-time economic performance and local investment efforts, rather than relying exclusively on historical trends. Given the complexity and inherent limitations of the current system, this report will underscore the importance of greater transparency and methodological improvements in the allocation of fiscal transfers.

The first four scenarios examine simple variables often included in fiscal equalization formulas, such as population size, land area, and gross regional product (GRP) per capita. For conciseness, calculations for these simple scenarios are included in the appendix. More complex scenarios incorporate adjustments for factors like population density, rural population size, and composite indices such as the Regional Wellbeing Index and the Development Trap Index. A poverty adjustment is also considered. Comprehensive scenarios allocate varying weights to these variables. Table 8 summarizes all the scenarios in a traffic light-style table, indicating which regions would get additional—or fewer—transfers under each scenario.

Table 8: Summary of Proposed Transfers Under Each Scenario

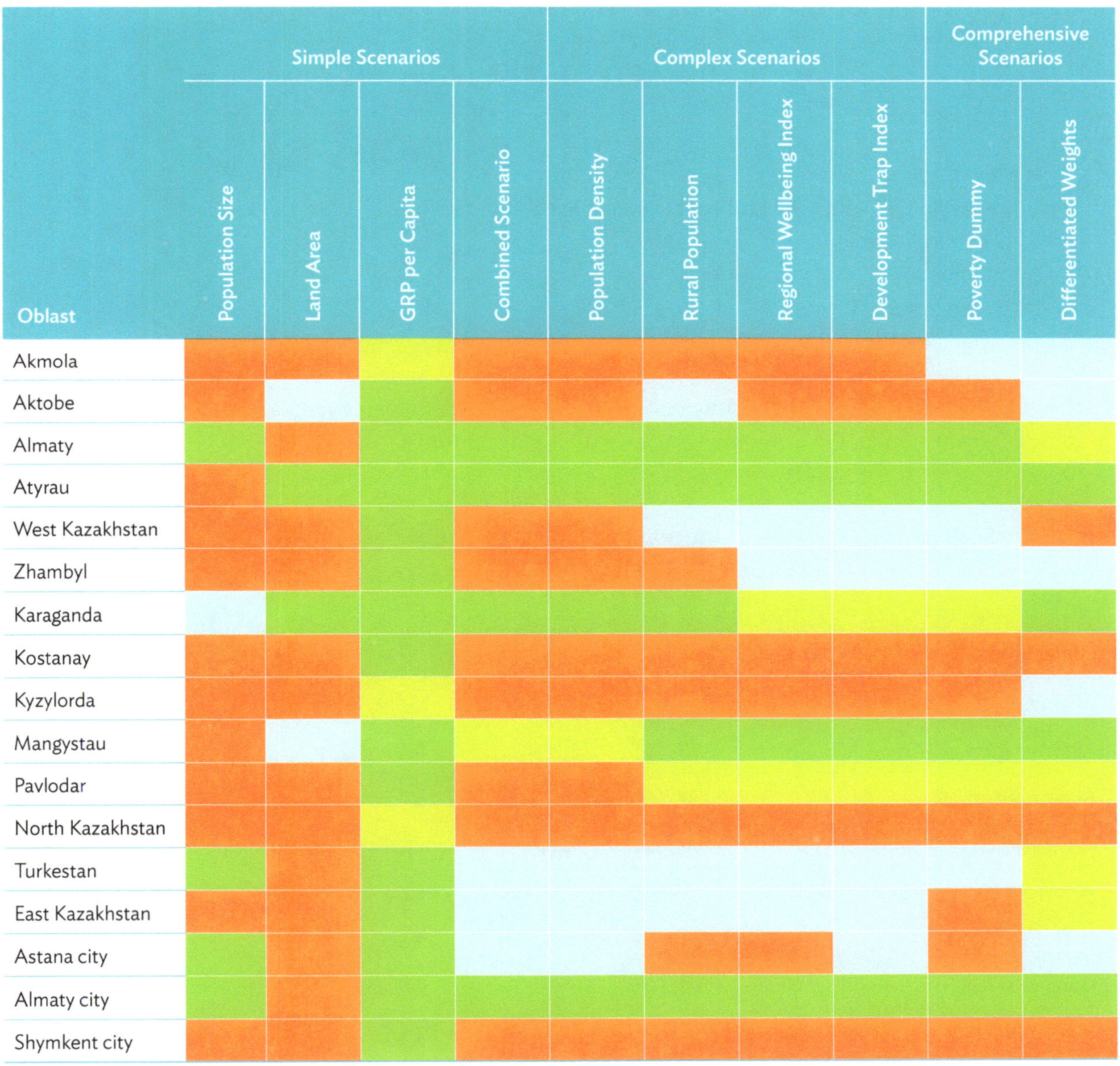

GRP = gross regional product.

Note: Light green indicates an increase of between 0% and 15%; light orange indicates a decrease of between 0% and 15%; darker green indicates an increase greater than 15%; darker orange indicates a decrease of more than 15%.

Source: Authors' calculations based on data from the Bureau of National Statistics of the Agency for Strategic Planning and Reforms of the Republic of Kazakhstan.

Given issues related to availability,[6] the analysis is based on 2021 data. The newly formed regions of Abay, Zhetisu, and Ulytau are not included in the calculations.

Simple Scenarios

Combined Scenario

To address the limitations of single-variable models, a combined scenario incorporates population size, land area, and GRP per capita. The formula for fiscal needs in this scenario is as follows:

$$\text{Fiscal needs}(i) = E_i(w_1 PI + w_2 LA + w_3 GRP)$$

where:

i = is a given *oblast*
w = is the weight (equal to 0.33 for each variable in this scenario)
E = total expenditure
PI = population index
LA = land area index
GRP = GRP per capita index

Each index is calculated using the same methodology as the single-variable scenarios. Table 9 presents the proposed transfers under this combined scenario, alongside current allocations.

Table 9: Proposed Transfers Under the Scenario Combining Population Size, Land Area, and Gross Regional Product per Capita, by Oblast

Oblast	Current Transfers (T million)	New Transfers (T million)	Difference (T million)
Akmola region	298,031	164,601	–133,430
Aktobe region	223,125	182,331	–40,795
Almaty region	427,157	602,841	175,684
Atyrau region	77,056	158,648	81,592
West Kazakhstan region	171,484	102,396	–69,088
Zhambyl region	368,259	248,421	–119,837
Karaganda region	301,625	391,216	89,591
Kostanay region	254,902	165,533	–89,369

continued on next page

6 The two indices employed in the analysis, namely the Regional Wellbeing Index and the Development Trap Index, are currently not available for the three new regions added in 2022.

Table 9 *continued*

Oblast	Current Transfers (T million)	New Transfers (T million)	Difference (T million)
Kyzylorda region	290,840	177,494	-113,346
Mangystau region	88,842	98,946	10,104
Pavlodar region	165,203	128,430	-36,773
North Kazakhstan region	278,066	118,339	-159,727
Turkestan region	757,603	673,854	-83,748
East Kazakhstan region	386,991	350,625	-36,365
Astana city	207,474	180,799	-26,675
Almaty city	174,336	438,957	264,621
Shymkent city	283,948	189,624	-94,324
TOTAL	**4,754,941**	**4,373,055**	**-381,885**

Source: Authors' calculations based on data from the Bureau of National Statistics of the Agency for Strategic Planning and Reforms of the Republic of Kazakhstan.

The combined scenario balances allocations across the three variables, reducing overall transfers by approximately 8%. Certain oblasts, such as Almaty city and Karaganda, see notable increases, reflecting their economic and demographic significance. Conversely, reductions occur in regions like North Kazakhstan and Zhambyl, where lower population density and GRP per capita result in decreased allocations.

This approach ensures a more nuanced distribution of resources, addressing demographic, geographic, and economic factors simultaneously, while mitigating the biases inherent in single-variable models. By combining these variables, Kazakhstan can create a more equitable and effective fiscal equalization framework, supporting balanced regional development. Appendix 1 presents additional simple scenarios.

More Complex Scenarios

Population Density

Building on the earlier scenarios, this section incorporates population density as an additional variable. The underlying assumption is that densely populated areas benefit from economies of scale in delivering public goods and services, thereby reducing costs. In contrast, sparsely populated regions incur higher costs to maintain equivalent service levels. The formula for this scenario is:

$$\text{Fiscal needs}(i) = E_i(w_1 PI + w_2 LA + w_3 GRP + w_4 PD)$$

where:

i = is a given *oblast*
w = is the weight
E = total expenditure
PI = population index
LA = land area index
GRP = GRP per capita index
PD = population density index

The model employs equal weights for all four variables; hence, w assumes the value of 0.25. The population density adjustment index is calculated using inverted, normalized scores based on regional population density relative to the national average (Table 10).

Table 10: Proposed Transfers with Population Density Adjustments, by Oblast

Oblast	Current Transfers (T million)	New Transfers (T million)	Difference (T million)
Akmola region	298,031	164,601	–133,430
Aktobe region	223,125	182,331	–40,795
Almaty region	427,157	602,841	175,684
Atyrau region	77,056	158,648	81,592
West Kazakhstan region	171,484	102,396	–69,088
Zhambyl region	368,259	248,421	–119,837
Karaganda region	301,625	391,216	89,591
Kostanay region	254,902	165,533	–89,369
Kyzylorda region	290,840	177,494	–113,346
Mangystau region	88,842	98,946	10,104
Pavlodar region	165,203	128,430	–36,773
North Kazakhstan region	278,066	118,339	–159,727
Turkestan region	757,603	673,854	–83,748
East Kazakhstan region	386,991	350,625	–36,365
Astana city	207,474	180,799	–26,675
Almaty city	174,336	438,957	264,621
Shymkent city	283,948	189,624	–94,324
TOTAL	**4,754,941**	**5,086,925**	**331,984**

Source: Authors' calculations based on data from the Bureau of National Statistics of the Agency for Strategic Planning and Reforms of the Republic of Kazakhstan.

Under this scenario, total allocations increase by approximately 7%, reflecting an adjustment in priorities. Turkestan region, with its high population density, receives T673,854 million, highlighting its role in national growth. Similarly, Almaty city, Kazakhstan's largest urban center, sees a significant increase to T438,957 million, emphasizing its importance in supporting urban infrastructure and economic contributions. Regions like Karaganda (T391,216 million) and East Kazakhstan (T350,625 million) also receive substantial allocations, reflecting their industrial significance and geographic size.

Conversely, regions such as Mangystau (T98,946 million) and Pavlodar (T128,430 million) receive smaller amounts. Shymkent city sees a notable decrease (T189,624 million), reflecting a shift away from prioritizing this urban area compared to Almaty and Astana.

This approach demonstrates a focus on regions with higher population density and developmental potential, while deprioritizing areas with fewer socioeconomic challenges.

Rural Population

The next scenario introduces rural population as an additional variable. The assumption is that regions with larger rural populations face increased costs in delivering public services to remote areas, a challenge common in countries with mountainous or sparsely populated regions, such as Switzerland. The formula for this scenario is:

$$\text{Fiscal needs}(i) = E_i(w_1PI + w_2LA + w_3GRP + w_4PD + w_5RP)$$

where:

i = is a given *oblast*
w = is the weight
E = total expenditure
PI = population index
LA = land area index
GRP = GRP per capita index
PD = population density index
RP = rural population index

Each variable is given an equal weight of 0.20. The rural population index uses normalized scores based on the share of rural populations in each oblast. Table 11 presents the proposed transfers under this scenario.

In this scenario, Turkestan region increases its allocation significantly, reflecting the need for investment to address poverty and developmental challenges in one of Kazakhstan's less economically developed regions. This aligns with the government's broader objective of reducing regional disparities and fostering balanced national growth. Substantial allocations to Karaganda and Almaty city further highlight a focus on supporting regions with significant economic and urban development needs. These areas are integral to Kazakhstan's industrial and economic strategy, requiring higher funding levels to sustain their growth and address pressing challenges.

Table 11: Proposed Transfers with Rural Population Adjustments, by Oblast

Oblast	Current Transfers (T million)	New Transfers (T million)	Difference (T million)
Akmola region	298,031	216,170	−81,861
Aktobe region	223,125	200,189	−22,937
Almaty region	427,157	645,739	218,582
Atyrau region	77,056	242,249	165,194
West Kazakhstan region	171,484	147,198	−24,286
Zhambyl region	368,259	297,403	−70,856
Karaganda region	301,625	361,574	59,949
Kostanay region	254,902	199,359	−55,543
Kyzylorda region	290,840	219,016	−71,824
Mangystau region	88,842	145,956	57,113
Pavlodar region	165,203	168,058	2,855
North Kazakhstan region	278,066	171,424	−106,642
Turkestan region	757,603	735,001	−22,602
East Kazakhstan region	386,991	365,998	−20,992
Astana city	207,474	160,286	−47,188
Almaty city	174,336	266,035	91,699
Shymkent city	283,948	176,541	−107,407
TOTAL	**4,754,941**	**4,718,195**	**−36,746**

Source: Authors' calculations based on data from the Bureau of National Statistics of the Agency for Strategic Planning and Reforms of the Republic of Kazakhstan.

In contrast, the reductions in funding for West Kazakhstan region and the modest increases for other resource-rich areas, such as Atyrau, suggest a deliberate shift in priorities. The new formula appears to balance resource wealth with other critical factors, including population, land area, and poverty levels.

However, significant reductions in funding for regions like Shymkent, Akmola, and Kostanay raise concerns about their capacity to address socioeconomic challenges effectively. Shymkent city experiences the largest decrease, with a reduction of T107,407 million relative to the current distribution funds, signaling a notable shift in priorities away from this urban area. Similarly, Akmola region faces a significant funding cut of T81,861 million, deprioritizing its fiscal needs relative to other regions. These reductions could impede these regions' ability to meet their development goals and tackle existing disparities.

Regional Wellbeing Index

In this scenario, the Regional Wellbeing Index (RWI) is introduced as a new variable for calculating fiscal needs. Developed by Rodríguez-Pose et al. (2024a) and continued by the Economic Research Institute, the RWI provides an aggregate measure of wellbeing across Kazakhstan's oblasts. It combines macroeconomic and subjective factors to offer a comprehensive assessment of regional wellbeing.

Incorporating wellbeing into fiscal allocation processes reflects global trends in budgetary policy. For example, New Zealand has pioneered the integration of wellbeing measures into national budgeting, embedding foresight-driven components into decision making (OECD 2024a). Similarly, many OECD countries now include wellbeing and inequality considerations at both the planning (ex ante) and evaluation (ex post) stages of their budgetary frameworks.

For Kazakhstan, including the RWI in fiscal allocation formulas ensures transfers address quality-of-life challenges alongside traditional economic and demographic factors. The formula for this scenario is as follows:

$$\text{Fiscal needs}(i) = E_i(w_1PI + w_2LA + w_3GRP + w_4PD + w_5RP + w_6RWI)$$

where:

i = is a given *oblast*
w = is the weight
E = total expenditure
PI = population index
LA = land area index
GRP = GRP per capita index
PD = population density index
RP = rural population index
RWI = Regional Wellbeing Index

The current formula now includes a total of six variables and each variable is given equal weight (roughly 0.17). The RWI values are inverted in this model, prioritizing regions with lower wellbeing scores by allocating them greater transfers. This ensures resources are directed toward areas with the most pressing socioeconomic challenges. Figure 18 visualizes the RWI scores across Kazakhstan's oblasts, while Table 12 portrays the proposed transfers under this scenario.

The proposed scenario is one of nuanced changes in fiscal allocations across regions. Turkestan region continues to receive the highest allocation (T716,795 million), reflecting its large population and developmental challenges. Atyrau also sees a significant increase in transfers (T127,396 million), marking a shift toward addressing broader socioeconomic needs beyond its resource wealth.

Conversely, North Kazakhstan faces the largest reduction (T135,270 million), reflecting relatively lower socioeconomic demands. Shymkent city also experiences a substantial decrease (T117,739 million), indicating a shift away from prioritizing urban development in this scenario.

Figure 18: Representation of the Regional Wellbeing Index, by Oblast, 2021

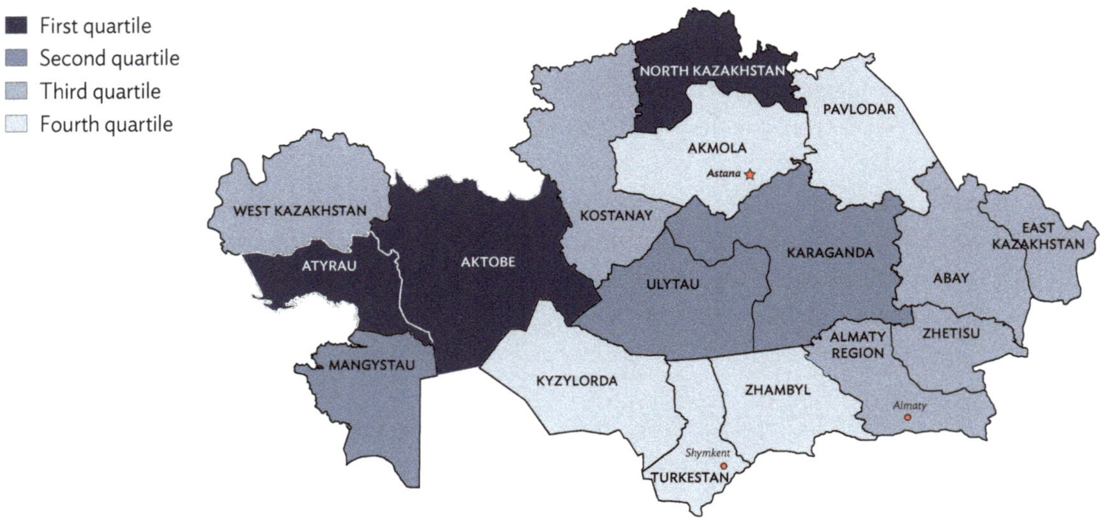

Source: Rodríguez-Pose et al. (2024a).

Table 12: Proposed Transfers with Regional Wellbeing Adjustments, by Oblast

Oblast	Current Transfers (T million)	New Transfers (T million)	Difference (T million)
Akmola region	298,031	221,485	–76,546
Aktobe region	223,125	174,426	–48,699
Almaty region	427,157	591,821	164,664
Atyrau region	77,056	204,452	127,396
West Kazakhstan region	171,484	146,130	–25,354
Zhambyl region	368,259	326,093	–42,166
Karaganda region	301,625	322,174	20,550
Kostanay region	254,902	200,393	–5,508
Kyzylorda region	290,840	197,438	–93,402
Mangystau region	88,842	138,626	49,784
Pavlodar region	165,203	185,797	20,594
North Kazakhstan region	278,066	142,796	–135,270
Turkestan region	757,603	716,795	–40,808
East Kazakhstan region	386,991	348,735	–38,256
Astana city	207,474	152,573	–54,901
Almaty city	174,336	251,255	76,919
Shymkent city	283,948	166,209	–117,739
TOTAL	**4,754,941**	**4,487,198**	**–267,742**

Source: Authors' calculations based on data from the Bureau of National Statistics of the Agency for Strategic Planning and Reforms of the Republic of Kazakhstan.

Development Trap Index

This scenario introduces the Development Trap Index (DTI), a measure assessing regions' risk of economic stagnation. Developed by Rodríguez-Pose and Bartalucci (2021) for Kazakhstan, the DTI incorporates metrics on productivity, employment, and economic diversification. Unlike traditional growth measures like GRP per capita, the DTI accounts for structural risks and diverse development trajectories, offering a nuanced tool for fiscal planning.

The formula for this scenario expands to include the DTI:

$$\text{Fiscal needs}(i) = E_i(w_1PI + w_2LA + w_3GRP + w_4PD + w_5RP + w_6RWI + w_7DTI)$$

where:

i = is a given *oblast*
w = is the weight
E = total expenditure
PI = population index
LA = land area index
GRP = GRP per capita index
PD = population density index
RP = rural population index
RWI = Regional Wellbeing Index
DTI = Development Trap Index

This scenario allows for the identification of regions nearing stagnation, regardless of their historical growth trajectories, enabling targeted support for at-risk areas. Figure 19 visualizes DTI scores across Kazakhstan's oblasts, while Table 13 presents the resulting fiscal allocations.

Figure 19: Average Risk of Being Trapped, by Oblast

Source: Rodríguez-Pose and Bartalucci (2021).

Table 13: Proposed Transfers with Development Trap Status, by Oblast

Oblast	Current Transfers (T million)	New Transfers (T million)	Difference (T million)
Akmola region	298,031	218,660	–79,371
Aktobe region	223,125	176,524	–46,601
Almaty region	427,157	569,319	142,163
Atyrau region	77,056	214,996	137,940
West Kazakhstan region	171,484	150,270	–21,214
Zhambyl region	368,259	317,265	–50,994
Karaganda region	301,625	311,081	9,456
Kostanay region	254,902	199,454	–55,448
Kyzylorda region	290,840	200,185	–90,655
Mangystau region	88,842	144,068	55,226
Pavlodar region	165,203	184,490	19,286
North Kazakhstan region	278,066	146,217	–131,849
Turkestan region	757,603	682,108	–75,495
East Kazakhstan region	386,991	339,519	–47,471
Astana city	207,474	185,151	–22,323
Almaty city	174,336	290,247	115,912
Shymkent city	283,948	176,153	–10,795
TOTAL	**4,754,941**	**4,505,707**	**–249,234**

Source: Authors' calculations based on data from the Bureau of National Statistics of the Agency for Strategic Planning and Reforms of the Republic of Kazakhstan.

Regions such as Turkestan (T682,108 million) and Atyrau (T214,996 million) emerge as significant beneficiaries, underscoring their diverse economic functions and developmental challenges. Almaty city also sees a significant increase, rising to T290,247 million, ensuring its capacity to address urban growth and infrastructure needs.

Conversely, Shymkent city faces the largest reduction (T107,795 million), reflecting a reassessment of its fiscal priorities. North Kazakhstan and Kostanay regions also experience significant cuts, highlighting a shift in focus toward other areas with higher developmental risks.

Regions like Karaganda and Pavlodar experience relatively stable allocations, with modest increases of T9,456 million and T19,286 million, respectively.

These scenarios demonstrate how nuanced fiscal planning can address developmental imbalances, ensuring equitable and effective resource distribution across Kazakhstan.

Comprehensive Scenarios

Poverty Levels

Finally, we present two comprehensive scenarios. The first comprehensive scenario integrates adjustments for regional poverty levels. Including poverty measures in equalization formulas is a common practice in developing countries, where disparities between urban and rural areas or among regions are often significant. This approach ensures resources are directed toward oblasts with higher poverty rates, addressing socioeconomic challenges and supporting balanced development.

The formula for this scenario expands on previous models by adding a poverty adjustment variable (POV):

$$\text{Fiscal needs}(i) = E_i(w_1PI + w_2LA + w_3GRP + w_4PD + w_5RP + w_6RWI + w_7DTI + POV)$$

where:

i = is a given *oblast*
w = is the weight
E = total expenditure
PI = population index
LA = land area index
GRP = GRP per capita index
PD = population density index
RP = rural population index
RWI = Regional Wellbeing Index
DTI = Development Trap Index
POV = poverty dummy

Regions with poverty rates above the national average—such as Akmola, Zhambyl, Kyzylorda, Mangystau, North Kazakhstan, Turkestan, and East Kazakhstan—receive additional transfers to address socioeconomic challenges associated with higher poverty levels.

Under this scenario (Table 14), Turkestan receives the largest allocation (T775,608 million), reflecting its demographic significance and the developmental challenges it faces. East Kazakhstan (T397,201 million) also benefits significantly, owing to its land area and diverse economic base. Atyrau sees a substantial increase (T137,940 million), highlighting a shift toward addressing broader socioeconomic needs beyond resource wealth. Almaty city also experiences a notable increase of T115,912 million, ensuring it can manage urban infrastructure and population growth.

Conversely, North Kazakhstan (T98,774 million) and Shymkent city (T107,795 million) face significant reductions, potentially limiting their ability to address fiscal needs. Regions like Zhambyl and Kyzylorda experience smaller decreases, reflecting a balanced approach to resource distribution.

Table 14: Proposed Transfers with Poverty Adjustment, by Oblast

Oblast	Current Transfers (T million)	New Transfers (T million)	Difference (T million)
Akmola region	298,031	259,389	–38,642
Aktobe region	223,125	176,524	–46,601
Almaty region	427,157	569,319	142,163
Atyrau region	77,056	214,996	137,940
West Kazakhstan region	171,484	150,270	–21,214
Zhambyl region	368,259	364,297	–3,962
Karaganda region	301,625	311,081	9,456
Kostanay region	254,902	199,454	–55,448
Kyzylorda region	290,840	236,607	–54,233
Mangystau region	88,842	171,987	83,145
Pavlodar region	165,203	184,490	19,286
North Kazakhstan region	278,066	179,292	–98,774
Turkestan region	757,603	775,608	18,005
East Kazakhstan region	386,991	397,201	10,210
Astana city	207,474	185,151	–22,323
Almaty city	174,336	290,247	115,912
Shymkent city	283,948	176,153	–107,795
TOTAL	**4,754,941**	**4,842,065**	**87,125**

Source: Authors' calculations based on data from the Bureau of National Statistics of the Agency for Strategic Planning and Reforms of the Republic of Kazakhstan.

Differentiated Weights

The second comprehensive scenario introduces differentiated weights to the formula variables, reflecting practices in advanced equalization systems such as Australia's CGC. In such systems, the weights assigned to variables often reflect political decisions and collaborative discussions among government levels.

In this scenario—and as an example of how to implement this method—we exclude the DTI owing to its potential to favor some high-income regions, such as Atyrau and Almaty city, which exhibit significant development traps. Instead, greater emphasis is placed on poverty levels (POV), which now carry a weight of 0.2. The formula is as follows:

$$\text{Fiscal needs}(i) = E_i(0.2 * PI + 0.2 * LA + 0.2 * GRP + 0.2 * PD + 0.1 * RP + 0.1 * RWI + POV)$$

where:

i = is a given *oblast*
E = total expenditure
PI = population index
LA = land area index
GRP = GRP per capita index
PD = population density index[7]
RP = rural population index
RWI = Regional Wellbeing Index
POV = poverty dummy

The adjusted weights increase the equalization effects, prioritizing regions with higher socioeconomic vulnerabilities (Table 15).

Table 15: Proposed Transfers with Differentiated Weights, by Oblast

Oblast	Current Transfers (T million)	New Transfers (T million)	Difference (T million)
Akmola region	298,031	281,398	–16,633
Aktobe region	223,125	193,623	–29,502
Almaty region	427,157	460,354	33,197
Atyrau region	77,056	188,747	111,691
West Kazakhstan region	171,484	140,209	–31,276
Zhambyl region	368,259	354,548	–13,711
Karaganda region	301,625	358,980	57,355
Kostanay region	254,902	196,490	–58,411
Kyzylorda region	290,840	279,216	–11,624
Mangystau region	88,842	196,947	108,105
Pavlodar region	165,203	175,658	10,455
North Kazakhstan region	278,066	204,463	–73,603
Turkestan region	757,603	768,390	10,787
East Kazakhstan region	386,991	472,518	85,528
Astana city	207,474	121,013	–86,461
Almaty city	174,336	283,830	109,495
Shymkent city	283,948	126,418	–157,530
TOTAL	**4,754,941**	**4,802,803**	**47,863**

Source: Authors' calculations based on data from the Bureau of National Statistics of the Agency for Strategic Planning and Reforms of the Republic of Kazakhstan.

7 For the normalized scores of the population density index, the three city regions—Astana, Almaty city, and Shymkent city—are excluded owing to their status as outliers within the distribution. These regions are instead assigned a population density index of 0.

Regions such as Atyrau (additional T111,691 million) and Almaty city (additional T109,495 million) emerge as significant beneficiaries, reflecting their socioeconomic importance. East Kazakhstan also sees considerable increases (T85,528 million), aligning with its geographical and economic characteristics.

Conversely, Shymkent city (T157,530 million) experiences the largest reduction, signaling a shift in priorities away from this urban area. North Kazakhstan (T73,603 million) and other regions with fewer socioeconomic challenges, such as West Kazakhstan, also see reduced allocations.

This approach underscores a deliberate emphasis on equity, prioritizing socioeconomic vulnerabilities over historical growth metrics. While resource-rich regions may face challenges in sustaining growth under reduced allocations, the adjusted formula aims to foster balanced and inclusive development across Kazakhstan.

The Equalizing Impact of the Proposed Scenarios

To evaluate the equalizing impact of the proposed scenarios, we analyze the relationship between current regional transfers and the socioeconomic variables used in the scenarios. These variables typically explain regional disparities and offer insights into how closely aligned transfer patterns are with socioeconomic challenges and opportunities. Table 16 presents a correlation matrix highlighting the influence of these variables on transfer levels across Kazakhstan's oblasts.

Table 16: Correlation Matrix Between Regional Transfers and Each of the Variables Used in the Scenarios

Variables	(1)	(2)	(3)	(4)	(5)	(6)	(7)	(8)	(9)
(1) Transfers	1.000								
(2) Population size	0.620	1.000							
(3) Land area	0.097	0.000	1.000						
(4) Rural population	0.413	−0.168	0.134	1.000					
(5) Population density	−0.189	0.499	−0.528	−0.714	1.000				
(6) GRP per capita	−0.627	−0.142	−0.134	−0.289	0.298	1.000			
(7) Development Trap Index	−0.434	−0.222	−0.396	0.050	0.260	0.290	1.000		
(8) Regional Wellbeing Index	−0.396	−0.083	−0.041	−0.467	0.338	0.571	−0.022	1.000	
(9) Poverty rates	0.825	0.376	0.014	0.740	−0.383	−0.543	−0.264	−0.425	1.000

GRP = gross regional product.

Source: Authors' elaboration.

The analysis reveals several key patterns in the relationship between transfers and socioeconomic variables. Population size is strongly correlated with transfers (0.620), underscoring the importance of demographic demand in driving funding levels. Regions with larger populations receive significantly more funding, reflecting the higher costs associated with providing public services and addressing population-driven demands.

In contrast, land area has a weak and near-zero correlation (0.097) with transfers, suggesting geographical size is relatively minor in determining funding allocations. This finding highlights the prioritization of population size and economic activity over geographical considerations in existing transfer systems.
Rural population exhibits a moderate positive correlation (0.413) with transfers, indicating that regions with higher rural populations tend to receive more funding. This aligns with the higher costs of service delivery in rural areas. Conversely, population density shows a moderate negative correlation (−0.189), implying densely populated regions receive lower transfers relative to sparsely populated ones.

Poverty rates demonstrate the strongest positive correlation with transfers (0.825). This indicates that regions with higher poverty levels tend to receive significantly more funding, reflecting a policy focus on addressing socioeconomic vulnerabilities. Similarly, GRP per capita is negatively correlated with transfers (−0.627), suggesting economically stronger regions receive less funding. This pattern supports the equalization agenda, ensuring wealthier oblasts do not receive disproportionate benefits.

The DTI and the RWI exhibit modest negative correlations with transfers (−0.434 and −0.396, respectively). This indicates that these variables only marginally influence funding levels, serving as complementary factors rather than primary drivers. However, their inclusion in future formulas could enhance the capacity of fiscal transfers to address structural disparities and wellbeing deficits more effectively.

To further evaluate the potential equalizing impact of the proposed scenarios, the correlation between transfers and key regional inequality measures is assessed under each scenario. These relationships for 10 scenarios, focusing on variables such as GRP per capita, poverty rates, the DTI, and the RWI, are represented in Figure 20.

The analysis confirms a consistently negative correlation between proposed transfers and GRP per capita. This means regions with lower GRP per capita receive higher transfers, demonstrating the positive equalizing effect of the scenarios on income disparities. Notably, Scenario 3, which is based solely on GRP per capita, shows the strongest correlation. This scenario emphasizes redistribution to poorer regions, making it particularly effective in addressing income inequality.

Proposed transfers are positively correlated with poverty rates in almost all scenarios. Regions with higher poverty levels receive more funding, reinforcing the objective of reducing socioeconomic disparities. However, Scenario 2, which is based solely on land area, exhibits a much weaker correlation with poverty rates. This outcome reflects the lack of direct targeting of economic vulnerability under that scenario.

For the DTI, the correlation with proposed transfers is consistently negative. This suggests the current transfer system does not provide sufficient support to regions classified as "trapped." Addressing this issue may require introducing conditional or earmarked transfers specifically designed to address structural bottlenecks in these regions.

Figure 20: Correlation Graphs Between Transfer Funds and Four Measures of Regional Disparities

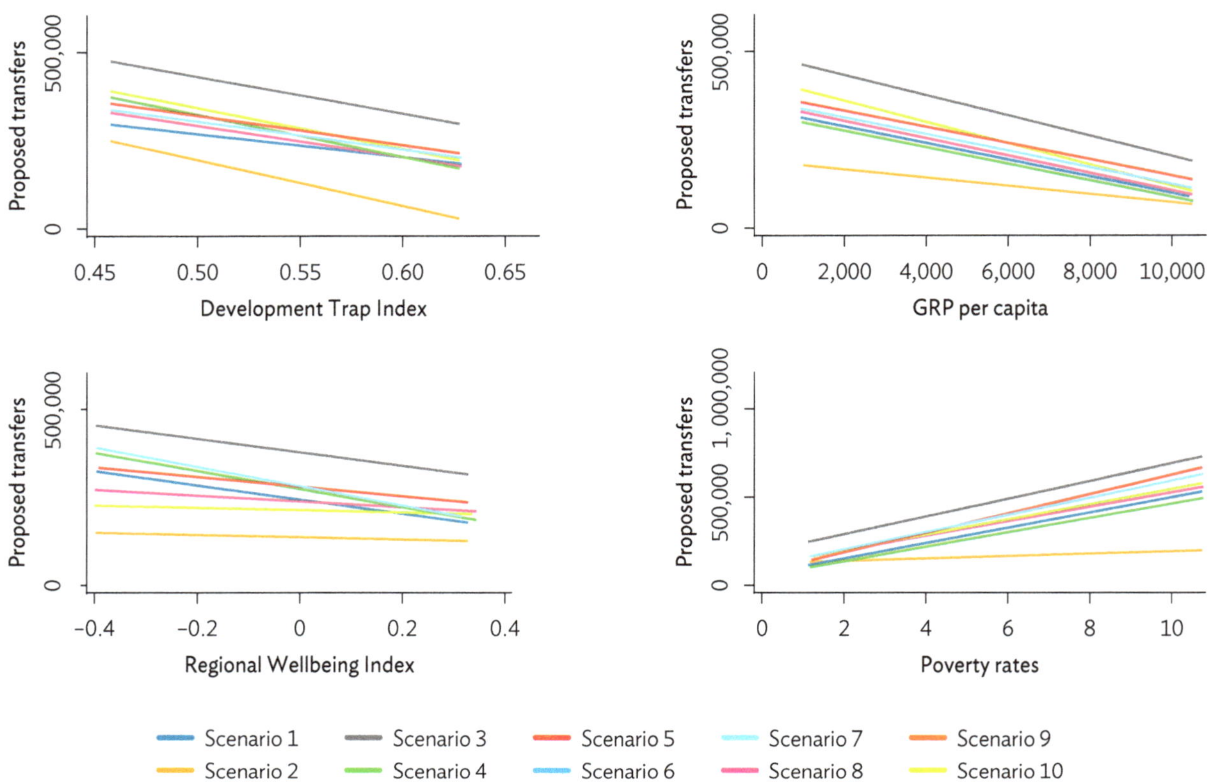

GRP = gross regional product.

Source: Authors' elaboration.

The correlation between proposed transfers and the RWI is also negative, though weaker than for other variables. This indicates that regions with lower wellbeing scores tend to receive more funding. However, the overall impact of the scenarios on equalizing wellbeing remains limited, likely because of the multidimensional nature of wellbeing and the diverse factors influencing it.

In summary, the proposed scenarios demonstrate strong potential to enhance fiscal equalization in Kazakhstan. By prioritizing regions with lower GRP per capita, higher poverty rates, and rural populations, the scenarios effectively address critical socioeconomic challenges. Nevertheless, targeted interventions, such as conditional transfers for development-trapped regions and strategies to improve wellbeing, could further enhance the effectiveness of fiscal policies in achieving balanced and inclusive development.

Limitations of Proposed Scenarios

While the proposed scenarios offer a comprehensive framework for reforming Kazakhstan's fiscal equalization system, several limitations must be acknowledged. These constraints underscore the importance of contextualizing the findings and recognizing the broader policy and methodological challenges influencing the analysis.

The first limitation lies in the methodology, which relies heavily on existing transfer levels and does not account for the fiscal capacity of regions. Incorporating a Representative Tax System (RTS) could provide a more accurate assessment of oblasts' revenue-raising potential. By evaluating the capacity of regions to generate their own revenues, the RTS would enable a more nuanced analysis of fiscal needs. However, implementing an RTS introduces significant complexity, requiring robust data availability and administrative capacity. This raises an essential trade-off between maintaining simplicity and transparency and achieving greater accuracy in the equalization system.

The second limitation concerns the reliance on 2021 data, which may not fully reflect the current fiscal landscape. Since the coronavirus disease pandemic, Kazakhstan has experienced substantial changes in regional expenditure patterns, including increased funding for economic recovery and public health. These shifts may have altered the relative needs of regions, potentially affecting the accuracy of the analysis. Regular updates to the data, conducted annually or more frequently, would ensure the continued relevance of the scenarios and their alignment with evolving fiscal realities.

A third limitation relates to the selection of variables and their assigned weights within the formula. The choice of which variables to prioritize and how heavily to weight them is inherently political, reflecting government priorities and strategic objectives. While the scenarios provide a structured framework, their outcomes are shaped by these decisions, which must align with national development goals. Policymakers must recognize that there is no universally "best" scenario; the optimal approach will depend on the extent to which the chosen variables and configurations support the country's overarching strategic priorities.

The final limitation involves the trade-offs inherent in designing an equalization system. While addressing structural disparities is a central objective, an overreliance on redistribution could unintentionally hinder the long-term development of resource-rich regions. Low allocations to these areas might encourage economic diversification and self-sufficiency, but they could also limit their ability to sustain growth, particularly if resource revenues decline. Similarly, urban centers benefiting from increased funding must ensure these additional resources are used effectively to improve infrastructure and living standards, avoiding inefficiencies or misallocations.

In conclusion, the proposed scenarios serve as a valuable foundation for exploring potential reforms to Kazakhstan's fiscal equalization system. Each scenario offers distinct advantages and insights, but their implementation will require careful consideration of methodological, political, and practical constraints. Ensuring these reforms achieve the desired outcomes will demand a balanced approach that addresses structural disparities while promoting sustainable growth and regional equity.

LESSONS LEARNED AND POLICY RECOMMENDATIONS 8

The analysis in this report highlights numerous international examples of fiscal decentralization and equalization systems that provide valuable lessons for Kazakhstan. Table 17 encapsulates the key policy recommendations, categorizing them by actions required at the central and subnational government levels. While some recommendations are specific to a single level of government, others require collaboration between the central and subnational authorities.

The successful implementation of fiscal decentralization in Kazakhstan will require coordinated efforts across all levels of government. A critical first step is for the central government to define clear spending mandates for oblasts, identifying responsibilities in areas such as health care, education, and infrastructure. Clear delineation of roles would minimize overlap and enable oblasts to manage their responsibilities predictably, enhancing governance and accountability. Brazil's approach to defining subnational government mandates provides a useful example, demonstrating how streamlined functions can reduce duplication and improve resource allocation.

Table 17: Summary of Main Policy Recommendations for Kazakhstan for Fiscal Decentralization and Equalization Across Different Levels of Government

Level of Government	Fiscal Decentralization	Fiscal Equalization
Central government	**Define clear spending mandates for oblasts** (e.g., education, health care) to minimize overlap and enhance accountability	**Implement a needs-based formula** that factors in several of the following indicators: population, poverty, infrastructure needs, wellbeing
	Introduce a fiscal responsibility law to avoid excessive regional deficits	**Adjust for natural resource revenue disparities** in equalization calculations
	Provide capacity-building programs to strengthen oblast governance	**Establish monitoring mechanisms** to assess the impact of equalization funds
	Publish detailed fiscal data to improve transparency and decision making	**Support economic diversification** through targeted equalization projects
	Think carefully about which taxes regions should retain, allowing regions to retain the revenues from certain local taxes, such as personal income tax and other highly visible and stable taxes	**Design a flexible but predictable equalization system** to address ad hoc crises
		Create an independent commission to oversee equalization transfers, ensuring transparency and reducing political interference; establish transparency in equalization allocation criteria

continued on next page

Table 17 *continued*

Level of Government	Fiscal Decentralization	Fiscal Equalization
Subnational government	**Build financial management** capacity to handle decentralized funds, investing in, among others, training on budgeting, accounting, and public financial management	**Prioritize high-impact investments in infrastructure, education, and health care**
	Develop local tax bases to reduce dependency on central funding	**Monitor socioeconomic outcomes** to ensure effective use of equalization funds
	Prioritize key service areas, focusing on critical services such as education, health care, and infrastructure to promote local development	**Use funds for sustainable initiatives**, prioritizing initiatives that build long-term economic resilience
	Foster public participation in budgetary decisions to enhance transparency and accountability	**Promote cross-oblast collaborations** for shared projects and economic integration and cooperation
	Explore the role of public–private partnerships: building collaboration between the public and private sectors can provide subnational governments with increased funds for underfunded spending areas	**Ensure involvement by subnational governments in decision-making**, and create the necessary civic spaces for regional governments to be involved in decisions pertaining to fiscal redistribution

Source: Authors' elaboration based on case studies presented throughout the report.

Fiscal stability at the subnational level must also be safeguarded. Implementing a fiscal responsibility law could help prevent excessive regional deficits by setting clear borrowing and spending limits for oblasts. Such laws have proven effective in maintaining economic stability in decentralized systems worldwide.

Building the capacity of subnational governments is essential as decentralization progresses. Capacity building programs should equip oblast officials with skills in budgeting, financial planning, and project management. These initiatives would empower subnational governments to optimize resource use, strengthen accountability, and deliver improved public services. Complementing this, the central government should mandate the publication of detailed fiscal data, ensuring transparency and enabling evidence-based decision making. Accessible fiscal information would support policymakers and citizens in scrutinizing budget allocations and expenditures.

Tax devolution is another critical element of fiscal decentralization. The central government must carefully decide which taxes oblasts should retain, prioritizing stable and visible revenue sources such as PIT. These taxes offer predictable revenue streams and enhance fiscal autonomy at the subnational level. Strengthening the fiscal capacity of oblasts will also prepare them for future tax collection and administration responsibilities.

Citizen involvement in budgetary processes can further enhance transparency and accountability. Participatory budgeting, as practiced in Brazil, has effectively aligned public services with community needs and improved government responsiveness. Kazakhstan could adopt similar mechanisms to make budget planning more inclusive and citizen-centric.

Fiscal decentralization must be complemented by a robust equalization mechanism to address disparities among regions. An effective equalization formula should consider variables such as population size, infrastructure needs, and poverty levels. This approach would direct resources to regions with the greatest developmental challenges, ensuring balanced national growth. Kazakhstan could also adopt a model similar to Canada's 50% rule, which adjusts equalization transfers based on natural resource revenues, ensuring resource-rich regions do not disproportionately benefit while poorer oblasts receive adequate support.

To ensure relevance, the equalization system should be flexible and regularly updated to reflect changing socioeconomic conditions. Monitoring mechanisms must accompany equalization funds to ensure their effective use in fostering long-term development goals.

Kazakhstan can leverage equalization funds to promote economic diversification. Norway's use of equalization funds to support innovation hubs and local industries offers a model for reducing dependence on central transfers. Kazakhstan could similarly target sectors such as technology, agriculture, and tourism in underdeveloped regions.

Establishing an independent commission to manage equalization transfers would enhance transparency and reduce political interference. Australia's CGC provides a valuable example of how an independent body can ensure fairness in fund distribution and build trust in the system.

Subnational governments must use equalization funds strategically, giving precedence to critical investments in health care, education, and infrastructure to improve quality of life and productivity. Encouraging oblasts to pool equalization funds for shared projects could enhance regional cooperation and economic integration. Collaborative efforts supported by the central government would maximize the impact of equalization funds, promoting equitable and sustainable growth across Kazakhstan.

Finally, it is equally important to consider how expenditure responsibilities are assigned among different tiers of government. Current data suggest the vertical share of total public expenditure for which subnational governments are directly responsible remains quite modest. As a result, even if transfers and tax devolution are improved, there is a risk that local authorities may still lack sufficient policy levers or budgetary clout to drive tangible development outcomes. If Kazakhstan's aim is to reap the full development potential of fiscal decentralization, reconciling more robust equalization with an expanded set of expenditure assignments will likely prove essential. Focusing on revenue reforms alone—without increasing the scope of local spending authority—risks yielding only partial benefits and may fail to generate the growth that the decentralization reforms are intended to achieve.

9 CONCLUSIONS

Since gaining independence in 1991, Kazakhstan has achieved remarkable economic growth, ascending international rankings and earning its classification as a middle-income country by the World Bank. However, this progress has been unevenly distributed, with growth concentrated in specific regions and sectors, leading to significant spatial imbalances. These disparities pose economic, social, and political risks, underscoring the urgent need for reforms that not only drive national economic growth but also unlock the potential of Kazakhstan's diverse territories. This report highlights the importance of fiscal decentralization and equalization as tools to address these regional inequalities while enhancing overall economic dynamism and growth.

As demonstrated throughout the report, fiscal decentralization and equalization often function as complementary mechanisms. Fiscal decentralization, which involves delegating taxing and spending authority to subnational governments, enhances local accountability, responsiveness to regional needs, and interregional competition, thereby fostering efficient public service delivery. Fiscal equalization, on the other hand, addresses disparities in fiscal capacities and expenditure needs across regions, enabling subnational governments to meet their obligations even when their own revenues fall short. International case studies and existing literature demonstrate the effectiveness of fiscal equalization in reducing fiscal inequalities, particularly in nations with high levels of fiscal decentralization.

Currently, Kazakhstan's subnational governments retain only a minimal share of tax revenues, primarily from property taxes and local fees. However, the central government has signaled its intent to further decentralize tax administration and collection. This shift would align Kazakhstan with the practices of higher-income countries, where subnational governments are gradually granted greater fiscal responsibilities. International examples, such as Brazil, the PRC, and Germany, demonstrate how fiscal decentralization can enhance efficiency and accountability in public expenditures. These cases also reveal how shared tax revenues promote accountability and encourage regional policy innovation in areas such as industrial development and welfare programs.

Also, reforms in the assignment of expenditure responsibility of local governments, as shown in the case studies presented in the Appendix, can enable a significant development effect in Kazakhstan too. This report has largely focused on the revenues side of subnational government finances. That said, considerable revisions in the expenditure responsibility of oblasts and raions are to be taken into account if subnational governments are given extra resources to fund the provision of public services.

However, the successful implementation of fiscal decentralization depends on certain preconditions. Enhanced financial management capacity and robust systems of checks and balances at the subnational level are essential. Without these foundational elements, the risks of decentralization—such as fiscal mismanagement and inefficiencies—could outweigh its benefits. Kazakhstan must therefore prioritize capacity-building initiatives as part of its fiscal reforms.

Equally critical is the need to improve the redistribution of funds across oblasts. A transparent, formula-based equalization system that is both flexible and predictable is vital. The international practices of countries like Australia, Canada, and Germany offer valuable lessons in this regard. Effective equalization systems often feature independent administration of funds, regular formula reviews, and mechanisms to account for fluctuations in natural resource revenues. Moreover, innovative budgeting approaches, such as wellbeing budgeting and green budgeting, are gaining prominence internationally. These methods shift the focus from traditional GDP metrics to broader measures of societal welfare and environmental sustainability. Kazakhstan could operationalize these concepts by incorporating wellbeing and environmental indicators into its transfer allocation formulas, ensuring alignment with both national and global development objectives.

To explore the practical implications of these principles, this report has presented 10 scenarios for fiscal redistribution. Categorized under "simple," "complex," and "comprehensive," these scenarios incorporate a range of variables, including population size, land area, poverty rates, and wellbeing indices. While most scenarios demonstrate significant equalizing effects, the ultimate choice of an optimal scenario depends on the government's strategic priorities. The selection of variables and the weights assigned to them are inherently political decisions that must align with Kazakhstan's broader development goals.

Greater synergies between fiscal decentralization, redistribution systems, and regional policies could yield substantial socioeconomic benefits at both national and regional levels. Fiscal transfers to lagging regions should address immediate fiscal gaps while fostering long-term economic growth. For instance, targeted transfers to development-trapped regions could stimulate economic activity, while earmarked funds could support initiatives that promote diversification away from resource dependence. This approach is particularly relevant for Kazakhstan, where an overreliance on natural resources has constrained economic resilience in many oblasts.

To ensure the success of these reforms, careful planning and transparent implementation are essential. Fiscal transfers must be accompanied by effective monitoring systems to enhance accountability and assess their impact. Empowering subnational governments and fostering regional autonomy will help create a more equitable system where no territory is left behind.

In brief, a well-designed combination of fiscal decentralization and equalization policies can serve as a cornerstone for Kazakhstan's sustainable development. If implemented effectively, these reforms will not only reduce regional disparities but also bolster the country's economic resilience and dynamism. Addressing structural inequalities is essential for enabling all regions to contribute to national growth. By doing so, Kazakhstan can lay the foundation for a more inclusive and prosperous future.

APPENDIX 1

Fiscal Decentralization Across the World: The Cases of Brazil, the People's Republic of China, and Germany

Fiscal decentralization has adopted a variety of forms across world. This section examines three such cases, focusing on how Brazil, the People's Republic of China (PRC), and Germany have tried to square the decentralization circle and exploring the impact of fiscal decentralization reforms on national and regional economies and identifying key success factors.

Brazil: Boosting Local Innovation in Welfare Programs

Brazil's fiscal decentralization system, one of the most comprehensive in Latin America, has also been instrumental in the country's economic and regional development. The adoption of the 1988 Constitution was the starting gun. It shifted Brazil toward a more decentralized federal structure and granted significant financial autonomy to states and municipalities. While this model has supported regional development and enabled subnational governments to tailor policies to local needs, it has also introduced challenges, including a rise in regional disparities and greater fiscal imbalances (Bird and Vaillancourt 1998).

The 1988 Constitution established Brazil's decentralization framework, which expanded revenue-sharing arrangements and empowered states and municipalities in areas such as education, healthcare, and infrastructure development (Serra and Afonso 2007). Subnational governments were granted autonomy over revenue generation and public spending, making Brazil one of the most fiscally decentralized countries in Latin America.

There are five key pillars underpinning Brazil's fiscal decentralization system:

- **Innovation in local governance and policy experimentation.** Fiscal decentralization has allowed Brazilian states and municipalities to innovate and experiment with policies, particularly in social services and public health. For example, São Paulo pioneered innovative health and education programs that were later adopted by other states, demonstrating how regional autonomy can promote policy innovation, while enhancing governance quality and social outcomes (Grin et al. 2021).
- **Autonomy in tax collection and spending.** Brazilian states and municipalities have significant autonomy to levy taxes, including the tax on circulation of goods and services (ICMS) at the state level and the services tax at the municipal level. This autonomy allows subnational governments to tailor tax rates and fiscal policies to meet local needs, promoting economic growth and enabling diverse public services.
- **Incentives for regional economic development.** Fiscal decentralization includes tax incentives aimed at stimulating regional development. Many states use ICMS reductions to attract investments, particularly in manufacturing and agriculture. This competition has spurred industrial growth in states such as São Paulo and Minas Gerais, which have become major industrial hubs owing to their proactive fiscal policies (Silva Rodrigues et al. 2021).

- **Revenue-sharing mechanisms.** Brazil's fiscal decentralization relies on complex revenue-sharing arrangements, redistributing federal tax revenues to state and municipal governments. Shared taxes, such as income tax, value-added tax (VAT), and taxes on industrialized products, are allocated through the State Participation Fund (FPE) and the Municipal Participation Fund (FPM). These mechanisms ensure equitable resource distribution, particularly benefiting less affluent regions (Silva Rodrigues et al. 2021).
- **Equalization transfers to address regional inequality.** Equalization transfers, like the FPE and FPM, aim to reduce disparities between wealthier and less-developed regions. These transfers channel resources to underdeveloped areas, especially in the north and northeast, funding essential services and infrastructure to promote more balanced growth (Silva Rodrigues et al. 2021).

Fiscal decentralization has contributed significantly to Brazil's regional economic growth, enabling states to use fiscal tools to promote local industries and attract investments. Industrialized states like São Paulo and Rio de Janeiro have leveraged their fiscal autonomy to foster the growth of manufacturing and services sectors, which contribute substantially to Brazil's GDP. São Paulo, for example, has implemented policies to attract investment in the automotive and pharmaceutical industries, creating employment and strengthening its regional economy (InvestSP 2024).

Devolution of fiscal powers to subnational governments has also encouraged innovation and experimentation in social programs, healthcare, and infrastructure development. One of the most notable examples is the Bolsa Família program. Initially designed and implemented at the municipal level, Bolsa Família provides direct cash transfers to low-income families. States and municipalities coordinate the program's implementation, tailoring it to local needs. The program has been credited with significantly reducing poverty and inequality in Brazil, with local governments being key for its success (Lindert et al. 2007).

In the Amazon region, states like Pará and Mato Grosso have used their fiscal autonomy to implement policies promoting sustainable agriculture and forest management. These initiatives, funded in part through state-collected revenues and international aid, incentivize farmers to adopt environmentally friendly practices. Such policies have contributed to reducing deforestation rates in the region, showcasing the innovative potential of fiscal decentralization (Assunção and Rocha 2016).

Curitiba provides another example of innovation at the municipal level. Leveraging local funds and fiscal autonomy, the city developed its Bus Rapid Transit (BRT) system, which is widely regarded as one of the most efficient public transport systems in the world. Curitiba's BRT model has since been replicated in cities across Latin America and beyond, demonstrating how fiscal decentralization enabled the city to address urban challenges effectively by providing innovative solutions that subsequently became widely adopted (Lindao et al. 2010).

Brazil's fiscal decentralization system has not only facilitated the development of local development strategies but also empowered subnational governments to address social and environmental challenges. For instance, fiscal autonomy enabled states like São Paulo to invest in innovative industrial policies while allowing northern states to focus on sustainable development. Similarly, Curitiba's ability to fund and design the BRT system highlights how fiscal decentralization can provide efficient solutions to local issues.

However, as in the previous cases, Brazil's fiscal decentralization system has encountered several challenges. Regional disparities remain significant, with economically weaker states heavily dependent on federal transfers. While mechanisms such as the FPE and the FPM are designed to reduce inequalities, their capacity and resources are insufficient to fully eliminate imbalances. To a considerable extent, poorer regions continue to rely on redistributions from wealthier states. Effectively addressing these disparities requires a delicate balance between fostering local autonomy and implementing robust mechanisms to ensure national cohesion.

People's Republic of China: Incentivizing Regional Autonomy for Economic Policy Implementation and Experimentation

The PRC's fiscal decentralization system has been a fundamental driver of its economic transformation since the late 1970s. The country decided to shift early fiscal responsibilities to subnational governments. This move enabled a more responsive governance and stimulated local economic growth across the PRC (Wang and Ma 2014). However, this system also introduced challenges, including regional inequalities and funding imbalances (Shen et al. 2012).

The PRC's fiscal framework operates as a tiered system, with the central government setting broad policies while subnational governments—including provinces, prefectures, and counties—take responsibility for implementation. Reforms initiated in 1978 marked the beginning of fiscal decentralization, allowing local governments to retain a significant share of tax revenues. This incentivized local economic development and empowered regional authorities to experiment with innovative policies (Cai and Treisman 2006).

Key components of the PRC's fiscal decentralization system include:

- **Autonomy in economic policy implementation.** Local governments enjoy substantial autonomy in applying national economic policies and developing local initiatives. This has enabled regions to experiment with policies and attract investment. Such autonomy has been critical to the PRC's economic success. For example, Shenzhen, designated as a Special Economic Zone (SEZ), evolved from a fishing village into a global technology hub through market-oriented reforms (Wang and Yang 2021).
- **A revenue-sharing system.** The 1994 tax-sharing reform established a revenue-sharing system that clarified tax authority between central and local governments. Tax revenues were divided into central, local, and shared categories, allowing local governments to collect business, personal income, and VAT revenues, which incentivized local economic growth (Wong 2000).
- **Fiscal competition among local governments.** Fiscal decentralization has encouraged competition among local governments to attract investment and boost gross domestic product (GDP). This was incentivized by the central government's cadre evaluation system, which tied local leaders' career progression to economic performance indicators like GDP growth. This competition drove rapid development and innovation, particularly in coastal provinces like Guangdong and Zhejiang, where thriving private sectors and industrial growth emerged (Jin et al. 2005).

The PRC's fiscal decentralization has been instrumental in its rapid economic ascent, transforming the country from an agrarian economy to an industrial powerhouse. Regional competition produced differentiated growth models and trajectories across provinces. Coastal regions like Jiangsu and Zhejiang attracted foreign investment, driving the PRC's export-led growth and generating significant employment opportunities (Jin et al. 2005). For example, Guangdong Province experienced annual GDP growth exceeding 10% from 1990 to 2010, underpinned by decentralized policies that attracted manufacturing and export industries (Cheng 2018).

However, fiscal decentralization also, at first, exacerbated regional disparities. In the early stages of decentralization, coastal provinces grew much faster than inland areas, widening income and opportunity gaps. In response, the central government introduced policies like the Western Development Strategy to channel investment into less-developed regions, addressing inequalities (Lin and Chen 2004).

Fiscal decentralization encouraged local governments to innovate and experiment, spurring technological progress and industrial development. For instance, Shenzhen leveraged its fiscal autonomy to attract technology firms, transforming into a hub for companies like Huawei and Tencent. This focus on innovation has significantly boosted the PRC's technology exports and global competitiveness (Harris 2017).

Local governments were allowed to issue municipal bonds to finance infrastructure and urban development. In Shanghai and Beijing, bond issuances funded transport and energy projects, laying the foundation for growth in the technology and industrial sectors (O'Brien and Pike 2015). Such projects created environments conducive to business and innovation, driving long-term regional growth.

In Jiangsu Province, fiscal autonomy facilitated its rise as a leader in renewable energy production. Local governments supported solar and wind energy firms through subsidies and grants, enabling companies like LONGi and JinkoSolar to thrive. This contributed to positioning Jiangsu as one of the main world hubs of green technology production (Wiedenbach 2021). Similarly, neighboring Zhejiang Province leveraged its fiscal autonomy to foster innovation ecosystems and entrepreneurship. Cities like Hangzhou became centers for technological innovation, exemplified by companies like Alibaba. Zhejiang's focus on creating a venture capital-friendly environment has driven high-value economic activities in the region (Xiaomin 2016).

In summary, the PRC's fiscal decentralization has been a cornerstone of its economic growth and regional innovation. The success factors—revenue-sharing systems, local autonomy, fiscal competition, and the development of SEZs—have enabled regions to pursue development strategies tailored to their specific needs. While decentralization has spurred growth and innovation, it has also intensified regional inequalities, requiring balancing and adapting policies from the central government. The PRC's experience underscores the potential of fiscal decentralization to stimulate localized growth and innovation while highlighting the importance on tapping on local potential as a viable way to address territorial disparities.

Germany: Promoting Local Fiscal Autonomy Through Shared Tax Revenues

Germany is widely recognized as a successful example of fiscal decentralization. Its federal structure enables a balanced distribution of financial powers among the federal, regional (*Länder*), and local governments. This system has facilitated balanced economic growth, reduced regional inequalities, and allowed tailored policies to address the specific needs of different regions (European Committee of the Regions 2024).

Germany's fiscal system is grounded in its Basic Law, which grants significant autonomy to the 16 *Länder* in areas such as education, law enforcement, and culture. Fiscal decentralization is supported by a framework of shared taxes and intergovernmental transfers. Major revenue sources include shared taxes such as income tax, corporate tax, and VAT, which are allocated among federal, regional, and municipal governments according to a predetermined formula. Local governments also raise revenue through property taxes and fees, but they depend significantly on transfers from higher levels of government to balance their budgets (Bury and Feld 2023).

Key features of Germany's fiscal decentralization system include:

- **A shared revenue system.** Taxes such as personal income tax, corporate income tax, and VAT are collected at the federal level and distributed among federal, *Länder*, and municipal governments. This guarantees stable revenue sources for all tiers of government and reduces the reliance of *Länder* on federal funds.
- **Fiscal autonomy for *Länder*.** The Länder have considerable autonomy in managing their budgets, levying certain taxes, and implementing regional policies. This allows them to tailor initiatives to their specific economic needs, such as education or cultural programs.
- **An equalization mechanism (*Länderfinanzausgleich*).** Wealthier states contribute funds that are redistributed to less affluent states to address economic disparities. This mechanism ensures all regions can provide comparable public services and infrastructure.
- **Debt regulation and fiscal responsibility.** Germany enforces strict debt rules through the "debt brake" policy (*Schuldenbremse*), limiting the borrowing capacity of governments. This policy, introduced in 2009, promotes fiscal discipline and financial stability.
- **Intergovernmental coordination.** Regular conferences and committees facilitate coordination between federal, regional, and local governments, ensuring cohesive national policies.

Germany's fiscal decentralization has contributed to regional economic resilience and innovation. During the 2008 financial crisis, different *Länder* implemented targeted fiscal measures to address regional challenges, aiding a swift national recovery (Baskaran and Feld 2013). States like Bavaria and Baden-Württemberg have successfully invested in education and technology, bolstering Germany's high-tech sector (Baier et al. 2013).

However, Germany's fiscal decentralization system is not without criticism. While it has generally been effective in narrowing economic disparities and ensuring comparable living standards across regions, it has been argued that the system reduces the incentive for economically stronger states to sustain high levels of revenue generation, as a portion of their revenue is redistributed (Bury and Feld 2023).

Fiscal autonomy at the regional level has contributed significantly to Germany's resilience during economic downturns. During the 2008 financial crisis, the *Länder* implemented targeted fiscal measures to address specific regional challenges, which was crucial for a swift and balanced national recovery (Baskaran and Feld 2013). The decentralized fiscal structure empowered local governments to act promptly and effectively, mitigating potential economic disruptions that could have impacted the broader national economy.

Overall, fiscal decentralization in Germany has enabled the *Länder* to design and implement policies that align with local preferences and economic conditions, thereby lifting regional economic growth.

Economically stronger states, such as Bavaria and Hesse, have been able to invest heavily in infrastructure and public services, attracting businesses and skilled labor to foster further economic development. Simultaneously, the *Länderfinanzausgleich* (equalization mechanism) has provided substantial support to economically weaker states, enabling them to enhance infrastructure, improve public services, and reduce regional inequalities (European Committee of the Regions 2024).

The cases of Brazil, the PRC, and Germany underscore the potential of fiscal decentralization to drive localized economic growth, trigger policy innovation, and enhance welfare. However, these experiences also highlight the risks of regional inequality and fiscal imbalance, underscoring the importance of robust equalization mechanisms like Germany's *Länderfinanzausgleich*.

APPENDIX 2

Fiscal Equalization Across the World: The Cases of Australia, Canada, and Germany

The success of fiscal decentralization across the world often hinges on a country's capacity to design a functional and fair fiscal equalization system. The following case studies from Australia, Canada, and Germany provide insights into the success factors of effective fiscal equalization systems in three of the countries that often serve as examples of well-functioning decentralization processes.

Australia: Ensuring Impartial Resource Allocation Through Independent Administration of Transfers

Australia operates one of the most sophisticated fiscal equalization systems globally. Its system is designed to ensure all states and territories can deliver comparable levels of public services regardless of disparities in revenue-raising capacity. Administered by the Commonwealth Grants Commission (CGC), this system has been key to maintaining economic stability, encouraging regional development, and promoting innovation. The equalization mechanism relies on redistributing goods and services tax revenue, which is pooled at the federal level and allocated to states and territories (CGC 2020). The CGC conducts detailed assessments of fiscal capacity, considering factors such as demographic composition, geographic features, and costs of service provision. Its objective is to enable each state to provide similar levels of public services while addressing disparities in revenue generation and cost burdens (CGC 2020).

Key Success Factors

- **Independent administration by the CGC.** The CGC operates autonomously, ensuring resource allocation decisions are based on objective data and methodologies rather than political influence (CGC 2020). This independence has been crucial in establishing trust in the system and increasing transparency, thereby enhancing the legitimacy of the equalization process. By maintaining impartiality, the CGC ensures decisions align with the principles of fairness and equity (CGC 2022).
- **Comprehensive assessment of needs and capacities.** The CGC employs a rigorous assessment framework to evaluate fiscal capacity and expenditure needs. This includes analyzing revenue-raising potential and cost factors such as population density, geographic isolation, and socioeconomic conditions. The process ensures resources are allocated equitably, enabling regions with lower fiscal capacity to provide services comparable to those in wealthier areas.
- **Flexible and regular adjustments.** The fiscal equalization process undergoes annual reviews to reflect changes in economic conditions, population shifts, and fiscal requirements. This adaptability guarantees the system remains effective over time, preventing resource allocation decisions from becoming outdated and enabling the system to respond to emerging challenges and opportunities (Shah 2017).

Outcomes

Fiscal equalization has been key in supporting economically weaker states, such as Tasmania and South Australia, allowing them to maintain public service levels essential to regional stability. These states benefit from higher per capita funding, which has been channeled into critical areas such as infrastructure, healthcare, and education. For instance, Tasmania has leveraged equalization funds to diversify its economy, focusing on expanding its tourism and agriculture sectors. This approach has created jobs and contributed significantly to regional gross domestic product (GDP) growth (Tasmanian Government 2024). Over time, these investments have enabled Tasmania to reduce its reliance on federal subsidies. The result has been greater economic autonomy.

The Northern Territory provides another persuasive example of the benefits of fiscal equalization. The territory has resorted to equalization funds to improve infrastructure in remote communities, enhancing access to essential services and stimulating local economies. These investments have been particularly impactful in addressing disparities between urban and rural areas. For example, equalization funds have supported projects that improve connectivity and service delivery in remote regions, thereby encouraging economic participation and reducing economic migration pressures (Morgan 2024).

Equalization has also driven broader socioeconomic benefits. By ensuring all regions, regardless of their fiscal capacity, can deliver comparable public services, the system has strengthened national cohesion and reduced the risks associated with uneven development. Moreover, the CGC's transparent processes have served as a model for other countries seeking to establish or refine their own fiscal equalization frameworks.

Canada: Balancing Flexibility and Stabilization for Resource-Dependent Provinces

Canada's fiscal equalization program is a cornerstone of its federal fiscal structure. It is designed to reduce economic disparities among provinces and ensure all Canadians have access to reasonably comparable levels of public services, regardless of provincial fiscal capacity. Established in 1957, the program is enshrined in the Canadian Constitution, which states its purpose as "ensuring that provincial governments have sufficient revenues to provide reasonably comparable levels of public services at reasonably comparable levels of taxation" (Canada Department of Finance 2006).

Unlike horizontal systems, where wealthier regions directly support poorer ones, Canada employs a vertical approach. Transfers are funded by federal revenues and directed to more vulnerable provinces with below-average fiscal capacities.

Natural Resource Revenue and Fiscal Capacity

As in Kazakhstan, natural resource revenues are central to Canada's tax collection. They are also fundamental in fiscal equalization. Provinces own their natural resources, leading to significant fiscal capacity variations between resource-rich provinces (e.g., Alberta and Saskatchewan) and resource-poor ones (e.g., the Atlantic provinces of New Brunswick, Nova Scotia, and Prince Edward Island). Historically, all resource revenues were included in fiscal capacity calculations. However, to balance development incentives and equalization goals, only 50% of resource revenues are now factored into the formula. This approach ensures resource-rich provinces are not excessively penalized while still addressing disparities in fiscal capacity (Dahlby 2008).

Key characteristics

- **Constitutional foundation.** Canada's equalization program benefits from a constitutional mandate, ensuring its continuity and adaptability over time. This legal backing provides stability and a clear framework for redistribution.
- **Dynamic formula and regular reviews.** The equalization formula is recalculated every 5 years, incorporating data on provincial revenues, expenditures, and population trends. This regular adjustment enables the program to adapt to economic fluctuations, particularly in resource prices (Government of Canada 2024).
- **Political flexibility.** The 50% inclusion rule for natural resources represents a political compromise, balancing the need for equity with incentives for resource development. This compromise has sustained provincial support for the program (Dahlby 2008).
- **Economic stabilization.** Equalization transfers provide financial stability to provinces during economic downturns. For instance, during the 2008 financial crisis and subsequent oil price collapse, Newfoundland and Labrador maintained public service levels thanks to equalization payments.

Canada's fiscal equalization system has been crucial in mitigating regional disparities, ensuring comparable public service delivery nationwide. Resource-dependent provinces benefit from a predictable revenue source that cushions the impact of economic shocks. For example, equalization has enabled more economically vulnerable provinces to maintain critical infrastructure, healthcare, and education investments, strengthening the long-term stability and growth of the country as a whole.

The program's adaptability and constitutional basis have been key to its success. By balancing the treatment of natural resource revenues and incorporating mechanisms to address fluctuating economic conditions, Canada's system supports innovation and development across provinces. Nonetheless, it faces political challenges, particularly regarding regional tensions between contributing and receiving provinces. Despite these issues, the equalization program remains an integral part of Canada's approach to buttressing national cohesion and economic equity.

Germany: A Four-Step Equalization System to Ensure Transparency and Stability

Germany's fiscal equalization system (known as *Finanzausgleich*) is among the most developed and comprehensive in the world, designed to ensure balanced economic growth and comparable living standards across its constituent states (*Länder*). At its core, the system aims to reduce disparities in financial capacity among the Länder by redistributing resources systematically through a four-step process.

First, taxes are collected at both federal and state levels, with income and corporate taxes shared among the federal government, *Länder*, and municipalities. This foundational revenue-sharing provides an initial layer of resources to all states. Second, vertical transfers are introduced, whereby the federal government directly transfers funds to states with fiscal capacities below a set benchmark, helping them reach a minimum baseline. Third, horizontal transfers are implemented, requiring wealthier *Länder* to contribute to the financial resources of less affluent ones, thereby reducing interregional disparities. Finally, for states that remain below the baseline fiscal capacity even after horizontal transfers, supplementary federal grants are provided to meet minimum financial standards (European Committee of Regions 2024).

Germany's Constitution—known as the Basic Law, or *Grundgesetz* in German—underpins this system, promoting the principle of "uniform living conditions," which mandates efforts to reduce regional disparities through fiscal equalization. This constitutional foundation ensures the system's legal robustness and minimizes political disputes over redistribution. The process is transparent, relying on well-defined formulas and benchmarks to calculate transfers, enabling states to plan their budgets with confidence and pushing forward cooperation among them. Furthermore, the system undergoes regular adjustments based on economic and demographic changes, ensuring its continued relevance. For example, a significant 2020 reform replaced parts of the previous horizontal transfer system with increased federal grants, streamlining redistribution and improving its efficiency.

Key Success Factors

- **Constitutional and legal framework.** Germany's fiscal equalization is grounded in its Basic Law, which legally mandates the reduction of disparities and ensures the system remains a stable and integral part of the country's governance structure.
- **Transparency and predictability.** The system employs clear, formula-based calculations for transfers, allowing states to anticipate funding levels and leading to a collaborative approach to redistribution.
- **Regular adjustments.** Reforms such as the 2020 overhaul demonstrate the adaptability of Germany's system, which evolves to address shifting economic and demographic dynamics.
- **Support for financially weaker states.** The equalization mechanism ensures even economically disadvantaged *Länder* can maintain essential public services and infrastructure, promoting social cohesion and stability nationwide.

Figure A2.1: Impact of Germany's Equalization on Per Capita Revenues

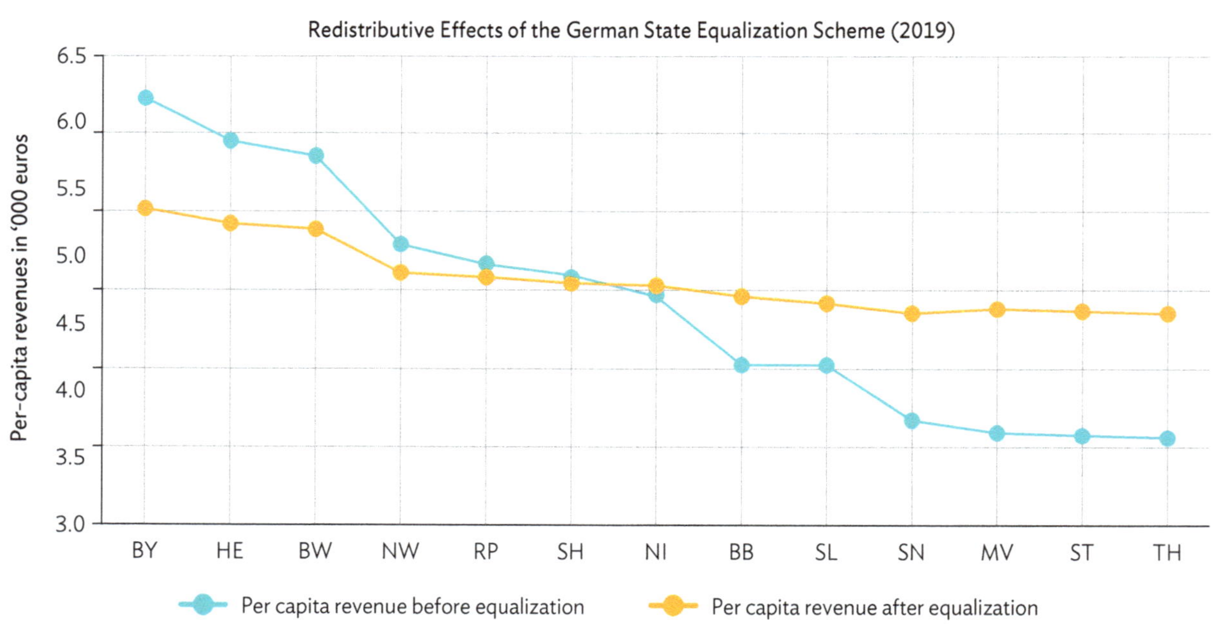

Source: Bury and Feld (2023).

Germany's fiscal equalization system has enabled weaker *Länder*—including those in the former East Germany—to provide equitable public services and pursue long-term development. These transfers have facilitated investments in critical sectors such as education, healthcare, and transportation infrastructure, reducing disparities and strengthening national unity. At the same time, the system has faced criticism, particularly regarding its potential to discourage economic self-improvement in recipient states and the political tensions it generates among wealthier, net-contributing states like Bavaria (Bury and Feld 2023).

Despite these challenges, the system remains a cornerstone of Germany's federal financial structure. Its success lies in its ability to balance equity with efficiency, supported by a robust legal framework and transparent processes. By enhancing cooperation and enabling sustained investment in weaker regions, Germany's fiscal equalization system is fundamental in reducing disparities and boosting economic and social cohesion. Figure A2.1 shows the system's impact on per capita revenues, highlighting its effectiveness in narrowing fiscal gaps across the different *Länder*.

APPENDIX 3

Additional Scenarios for Fiscal Equalization

Population Size

Population size is often used in fiscal equalization formulas to calculate a region's fiscal needs. It serves as a straightforward, measurable proxy for demand for public services, making it a widely adopted indicator in equalization systems worldwide. Countries such as Australia, Brazil, Germany, India, Japan, and South Africa include population size in their fiscal formulas. A larger population is typically associated with higher costs for delivering public goods and services, including education, infrastructure, and law enforcement.

In this scenario, fiscal needs are calculated using the following formula: Fiscal needs(i) = $E_i(w_1 PI)$

where:
i = is a given *oblast*
w = is the weight
E = total expenditure
PI = population index

In this case, we attribute w the value of 1, meaning that population variation is the sole criterion used to redistribute transfers across oblasts. Given the large variation across oblasts, the population index is the result of a normalized score calculated for each oblast (Table A3.1).

The results show that transfers using population as the sole redistribution criterion would flow primarily to regions with larger populations, such as Almaty city, Almaty region, and Turkestan, which together represent over 30% of Kazakhstan's population. In contrast, regions like Akmola, Atyrau, Mangystau, and North Kazakhstan would experience significant reductions in funding. A key advantage of using population size is its objectivity, as it cannot be easily manipulated by subnational governments. However, this simple model fails to account for other demographic and socioeconomic factors, such as income levels or living standards, which can significantly influence a region's fiscal needs.

Land Area

Land area is another widely used variable in equalization formulas, reflecting the greater costs associated with providing public goods and services in larger and often sparsely populated territories. A larger area typically requires more extensive infrastructure, such as roads, schools, and hospitals, to ensure adequate service delivery.

This scenario calculates fiscal needs using the following formula: Fiscal needs(i) = $E_i(w_1 LA)$

where:
i = is a given *oblast*
w = is the weight
E = total expenditure
LA = land area index

Table A3.1: Proposed Transfers by Oblast (population size)

Oblast	Current Transfers (T million)	New Transfers (T million)	Difference (T million)
Akmola region	298,031	50,786	−247,245
Aktobe region	223,125	79,513	−143,613
Almaty region	427,157	757,523	330,366
Atyrau region	77,056	32,307	−44,749
West Kazakhstan region	171,484	21,342	−150,142
Zhambyl region	368,259	181,432	−186,826
Karaganda region	301,625	289,639	−11,985
Kostanay region	254,902	76,652	−178,250
Kyzylorda region	290,840	61,561	−229,279
Mangystau region	88,842	27,790	−61,052
Pavlodar region	165,203	47,218	−117,985
North Kazakhstan region	278,066	21,181	−256,885
Turkestan region	757,603	910,361	152,758
East Kazakhstan region	386,991	314,188	−72,802
Astana city	207,474	240,045	32,571
Almaty city	174,336	852,289	677,954
Shymkent city	283,948	152,114	−131,834
Total	**4,754,940**	**4,115,942**	**−638,999**

Source: Authors' calculations based on data from the Bureau of National Statistics of the Agency for Strategic Planning and Reforms of the Republic of Kazakhstan.

As with population size, we attribute *w* the value of 1. Moreover, we normalize the values representing the percentage of an oblast's land area out of the total national land area (Table A3.2).

Larger regions, such as Atyrau and Karaganda, experience a notable increase in funding under a scenario based solely on territory. For instance, Karaganda region gains an additional T225,434 million compared to the current allocation, reflecting the formula's emphasis on land size. Conversely, densely populated or economically vital regions like Almaty city and Shymkent city face significant funding reductions. Almaty city's allocation decreases by T158,374 million, while Shymkent city suffers an even steeper decline of T283,641 million, almost eliminating its allocation.

Table A3.2: Proposed Transfers by Oblast (land area)

Oblast	Current Transfers (T million)	New Transfers (T million)	Difference (T million)
Akmola region	298,031	107,842	–190,189
Aktobe region	223,125	196,498	–26,627
Almaty region	427,157	316,070	–111,086
Atyrau region	77,056	108,234	31,178
West Kazakhstan region	171,484	81,601	–89,883
Zhambyl region	368,259	122,858	–245,401
Karaganda region	301,625	527,059	225,434
Kostanay region	254,902	128,414	–126,488
Kyzylorda region	290,840	149,350	–141,490
Mangystau region	88,842	83,774	–5,068
Pavlodar region	165,203	78,980	–86,223
North Kazakhstan region	278,066	58,535	–219,531
Turkestan region	757,603	196,628	–560,975
East Kazakhstan region	386,991	296,632	–90,359
Astana city	207,474	403	–207,070
Almaty city	174,336	15,962	–158,374
Shymkent city	283,948	307	–283,641
Total	**4,754,940**	**2,469,146**	**–2,285,794**

Source: Authors' calculations based on data from the Bureau of National Statistics of the Agency for Strategic Planning and Reforms of the Republic of Kazakhstan.

This scenario favors sparsely populated, geographically expansive regions at the expense of smaller or urbanized areas. This approach risks exacerbating regional inequalities, as more populous regions, with greater infrastructure and service demands, receive more limited support. For example, Mangystau sees only a minor reduction of T5,065 million, suggesting the formula's limited effect in such cases despite their considerable land area. While the formula simplifies the allocation process by concentrating on land size, it risks overlooking the complex needs of regions with high population densities or significant economic roles.

Gross Regional Product Per Capita

Macroeconomic variables such as per capita income and poverty levels are widely used in fiscal needs calculations, particularly in developing countries like Brazil, India, and Indonesia, where such metrics are integral to equalization formulas. In Kazakhstan, a similar approach can be applied by incorporating gross regional product (GRP) per capita into the formula for fiscal transfers.

The third single-variable scenario uses the following formula to determine fiscal needs:

$$\text{Fiscal needs}(i) = E_i(w_1 GRP)$$

where:

i = is a given *oblast*
w = is the weight (set to 1 in this scenario)
E = total expenditure
GRP = GRP per capita index

The GRP index is calculated using inverted, normalized shares of regional GRP per capita levels relative to the national average. Regions with higher per capita GRP receive lower equalizing transfers under this model (Table A3.3).

Table A3.3: Proposed Transfers by Oblast (gross regional product)

Oblast	Current Transfers (T million)	New Transfers (T million)	Difference (T million)
Akmola region	298,031	340,163	42,132
Aktobe region	223,125	276,506	53,381
Almaty region	427,157	732,701	305,544
Atyrau region	77,056	340,209	263,153
West Kazakhstan region	171,484	207,349	35,864
Zhambyl region	368,259	448,502	80,243
Karaganda region	301,625	368,804	67,180
Kostanay region	254,902	296,550	41,648
Kyzylorda region	290,840	326,949	36,109
Mangystau region	88,842	188,271	99,429
Pavlodar region	165,203	262,984	97,781
North Kazakhstan region	278,066	278,888	822
Turkestan region	757,603	934,994	177,391
East Kazakhstan region	386,991	451,680	64,690
Astana city	207,474	307,427	99,954
Almaty city	174,336	461,922	287,587
Shymkent city	283,948	422,197	138,249
Total	**4,754,940**	**6,646,097**	**1,891,156**

Source: Authors' calculations based on data from the Bureau of National Statistics of the Agency for Strategic Planning and Reforms of the Republic of Kazakhstan.

Under this formula, every region sees increased funding, though the magnitude varies. Regions such as Kyzylorda see modest increases (T36,109 million), while others, like Almaty region and Atyrau, accrue substantial gains (T305,544 million and T263,153 million, respectively). Urban centers such as Almaty and Shymkent also receive significant boosts, likely reflecting their centrality for national economic development. By increasing transfers across the board, this approach aims to enhance resources in all oblasts, potentially leading to a balanced national growth and cohesion, although potentially adding pressures to balance national budgets.

APPENDIX 4

Redistribution of Tax Revenues to the Budget Between the Levels of the Budget System

Current Provisions of the Budget Code (effective from 4 December 2008, No. 95-IV)	**Draft of the New Budget Code** (posted on the website of the Majilis of the Parliament of the Republic of Kazakhstan, dated 28 September 2023: https://mazhilis.parlam.kz/#/all-bill/pending-majilis)
Tax revenues to the republican budget	
Article 49. Receipts to the republican budget 1. Tax revenues to the republican budget are: □ CIT [corporate income tax] from business entities according to the list approved by the central authorized body for state planning together with the central authorized body for budget execution, except for receipts from oil sector organizations;	Article 26. Receipts to the republican budget 1. Tax revenues to the republican budget are: □ CIT according to the list of business entities determined by the central authorized body on budget policy, except for revenues from oil sector organizations; *The list of business entities stipulated in paragraph one of this subparagraph shall be approved by the central authorized body in charge of budget policy together with the central authorized body in charge of budget execution not later than 1 May of the year of completion of the current law on general transfers and shall not be subject to change during the period of validity of the law on general transfers.*
□ VAT [value-added tax], including on goods produced, work performed and services rendered in the territory of the Republic of Kazakhstan, and on goods imported into the territory of the Republic of Kazakhstan;	□ VAT, including on goods produced, work performed and services rendered in the territory of the Republic of Kazakhstan, and on goods imported into the territory of the Republic of Kazakhstan;
□ excise taxes on goods imported into the territory of the Republic of Kazakhstan in accordance with the legislation of the Republic of Kazakhstan; □ excise taxes on crude oil, gas condensate; □ gambling tax; □ excess profit tax, except for revenues from oil sector organizations; □ bonuses, except for receipts from oil sector organizations; □ mining tax, except for receipts from oil sector organizations; □ rent tax on exports, except for revenues from oil sector organizations; □ share of RK on the division of products under concluded contracts, except for receipts from oil sector organizations;	□ excise taxes on goods imported into the territory of the Republic of Kazakhstan in accordance with the legislation of the Republic of Kazakhstan; □ gambling tax; □ bonuses, except for receipts from oil sector organizations; □ mining tax, **except for common mineral resources, groundwater, therapeutic mud** and revenues from oil sector organizations; □ rent tax on exports, except for revenues from oil sector organizations; □ fee for the passage of motor vehicles through the territory of the Republic of Kazakhstan; □ fee for issuing permits for the use of radio spectrum to television and radio broadcasting organizations;

continued on next page

Table *continued*

Current Provisions of the Budget Code (effective from 4 December 2008, No. 95-IV)	**Draft of the New Budget Code** (posted on the website of the Majilis of the Parliament of the Republic of Kazakhstan, dated 28 September 2023: https://mazhilis.parlam.kz/#/all-bill/pending-majilis)
◻ additional payment by a subsoil user operating under a contract on production sharing, except for receipts from oil sector organizations; ◻ fee for the passage of motor vehicles through the territory of the Republic of Kazakhstan; ◻ fee for issuing permits for the use of radio spectrum to television and radio broadcasting organizations; ◻ fee for registration of a TV channel, radio channel, periodical print edition, news agency and network edition; ◻ fee for state registration of medicinal products and medical devices, as well as their re-registration; ◻ payment for provision of long-distance and (or) international telephone communication, as well as cellular communication; ◻ payment for the use of the radio frequency spectrum; ◻ digital mining fees; ◻ advance payments made in accordance with the customs legislation of the [Eurasian Economic Union] EAEU and the Republic of Kazakhstan on (customs duties on imported and exported goods; customs duties paid in accordance with the customs legislation of the Republic of Kazakhstan; special, anti-dumping, countervailing duties paid in connection with the application of measures to protect the domestic market), duties account of payment of forthcoming payments as well as value added tax and excise on goods imported into the customs territory of the EAEU; ◻ consular fee; ◻ state duty for affixing an apostille on official documents executed in the Republic of Kazakhstan by state bodies authorized by the Government of the Republic of Kazakhstan in accordance with an international treaty ratified by the Republic of Kazakhstan; ◻ fee for state registration of space objects and rights thereto;	◻ fee for registration of a TV channel, radio channel, periodical print edition, news agency and network edition; ◻ fee for state registration of medicinal products and medical devices, as well as their re-registration; ◻ payment for provision of long-distance and (or) international telephone communication, as well as cellular communication; ◻ payment for the use of the radio frequency spectrum; ◻ digital mining fees; ◻ advance payments made in accordance with the customs legislation of the EAEU and the Republic of Kazakhstan on account of payment of forthcoming payments (customs duties on imported and exported goods; customs duties paid in accordance with the customs legislation of the Republic of Kazakhstan; special, anti-dumping, countervailing duties paid in connection with the application of measures to protect the domestic market), as well as value added tax and excise duties on goods imported into the customs territory of the EAEU; ◻ consular fee; ◻ state duty for affixing an apostille on official documents executed in the Republic of Kazakhstan by state bodies authorized by the Government of the Republic of Kazakhstan in accordance with an international treaty ratified by the Republic of Kazakhstan; ◻ fee for state registration of space objects and rights thereto; ◻ fee for issuance of certificates issued by an authorized organization in the field of civil aviation for compliance with certification requirements established by the laws of the Republic of Kazakhstan regulating the use of airspace of the Republic of Kazakhstan and aviation activities; ◻ fee for issuance of authorization documents, consents for participants in the banking and insurance markets;

continued on next page

Table *continued*

Current Provisions of the Budget Code (effective from 4 December 2008, No. 95-IV)	Draft of the New Budget Code (posted on the website of the Majilis of the Parliament of the Republic of Kazakhstan, dated 28 September 2023: https://mazhilis.parlam.kz/#/all-bill/pending-majilis)
▫ fee for issuance of certificates issued by an authorized organization in the field of civil aviation for compliance with certification requirements established by the laws of the Republic of Kazakhstan on the use of airspace of the Republic of Kazakhstan and aviation activities; ▫ fee for issuance of authorization documents, consents for participants in the banking and insurance markets; ▫ license fee for the issuance of a license related to the right to engage in certain hydrocarbon activities; ▫ fee for issuance of a document confirming the residency of a foreigner or stateless person who is an investment resident of the International Financial Center "Astana".	▫ license fee for the issuance of a license related to the right to engage in certain hydrocarbon activities; ▫ fee for issuance of a document confirming the residency of a foreigner or stateless person who is an investment resident of the International Financial Center "Astana"; ▫ **payment for the use of specially protected natural territories of republican significance.**
Tax revenues to the budget of the city of republican significance, capital city	
Article 51. Receipts to the budgets of the city of republican significance, capital city 1. Tax revenues to the budgets of the city of republican significance, the capital are: ▫ PIT [personal income tax]; ▫ CIT, except for receipts from business entities according to the list approved by the central authorized body for state planning together with the central authorized body for budget execution, and receipts from oil sector organizations; ▫ social tax; ▫ property tax on individuals and legal entities, individual entrepreneurs; ▫ land tax; ▫ unified land tax; ▫ vehicle tax; ▫ excise taxes on: • all types of alcohol produced on the territory of the Republic of Kazakhstan; • alcoholic beverages produced in the territory of the Republic of Kazakhstan;	Article 27. Receipts to the budget of the city of republican significance, capital city 1. Tax revenues to the budget of the city of republican significance, the capital are: ▫ PIT; ▫ CIT, except for receipts from business entities according to the list determined and approved in accordance with subparagraph (1) of paragraph 1 of Article 26 of this Code, and receipts from oil sector organizations; ▫ social tax; ▫ property tax on individuals and legal entities, individual entrepreneurs; ▫ land tax; ▫ unified land tax; ▫ vehicle tax; ▫ excise taxes on: • all types of alcohol produced on the territory of the Republic of Kazakhstan; • alcoholic beverages produced in the territory of the Republic of Kazakhstan;

continued on next page

Table *continued*

Current Provisions of the Budget Code (effective from 4 December 2008, No. 95-IV)	**Draft of the New Budget Code** (posted on the website of the Majilis of the Parliament of the Republic of Kazakhstan, dated 28 September 2023: https://mazhilis.parlam.kz/#/all-bill/pending-majilis)
• beer with a volumetric content of ethyl alcohol not exceeding 0.5%, produced on the territory of the Republic of Kazakhstan; • tobacco products manufactured in the territory of the Republic of Kazakhstan; • passenger cars (except for cars with manual control or manual control adapter specially designed for persons with disabilities) manufactured in the territory of the Republic of Kazakhstan; • gasoline (except jet fuel), diesel fuel, gasohol, benzanol, nephras, light hydrocarbon blends and ecological fuel; □ payment for the use of water resources of surface sources; □ payment for forest uses; □ payment for negative impact on the environment; □ payment for the use of wildlife; □ payment for the use of land plots; □ fee for the right to engage in certain types of activities (fee for issuing licenses to engage in certain types of activities); □ fees for the use of licenses to engage in certain types of activities; □ fee for state (accounting) registration of legal entities, their branches and representative offices, except for commercial organizations, as well as their re-registration; □ state duty, except for consular fees and state duties credited to the republican budget; □ fee for state registration of pledge of movable property and mortgage of the vessel, as well as state registration of irrevocable authorization for deregistration and removal of the aircraft; □ fee for state registration of vehicles, as well as their re-registration; □ payment for placement of outdoor (visual) advertising in the open space outside the premises in the city of republican significance, the capital, in the right-of-way of public highways passing through the territory of the city of republican significance, the capital;	• beer products with a volume content of ethyl alcohol not exceeding 0.5%, produced in the territory of the Republic of Kazakhstan; • tobacco products manufactured in the territory of the Republic of Kazakhstan; • passenger cars (except for cars with manual control or manual control adapter specially designed for persons with disabilities) manufactured in the territory of the Republic of Kazakhstan; • gasoline (except jet fuel), diesel fuel, gasohol, benzanol, nephras, light hydrocarbon blend and ecological fuel; □ payment for the use of water resources of surface sources; □ payment for forest uses; □ payment for the use of wildlife; □ payment for the use of land plots; □ fee for the right to engage in certain types of activities (fee for issuing licenses to engage in certain types of activities); □ fees for the use of licenses to engage in certain types of activities; □ fee for state (accounting) registration of legal entities, their branches and representative offices, except for commercial organizations, as well as their re-registration; □ state duty, except for consular fees and state duties credited to the republican budget; □ fee for state registration of pledge of movable property and vessel mortgage, as well as state registration of irrevocable authorization for deregistration and removal of the aircraft; □ fee for state registration of vehicles, as well as their re-registration; □ payment for placement of outdoor (visual) advertising in the open space outside the premises in the city of republican significance, the capital, in the right-of-way of public highways passing through the territory of the city of republican significance, the capital; □ fee for issuance or extension of a permit to hire foreign labor in the RK;

continued on next page

Table *continued*

Current Provisions of the Budget Code (effective from 4 December 2008, No. 95-IV)	**Draft of the New Budget Code** (posted on the website of the Majilis of the Parliament of the Republic of Kazakhstan, dated 28 September 2023: https://mazhilis.parlam.kz/#/all-bill/pending-majilis)
◻ fee for issuance or extension of a permit to hire foreign labor in the RK; ◻ payment for reimbursement of historical costs.	◻ payment for reimbursement of historical costs; ◻ **mining tax on commonly occurring minerals, groundwater and therapeutic mud;** ◻ **payment for the use of specially protected natural territories of local significance;** ◻ **payment for the use of plant resources in the order of special use of plant life.**
Tax revenues to the regional budget	
Article 50. Receipts to the regional budget 1. Tax revenues to the regional budget are: ◻ PIT according to the norms of income distribution established by the regional maslikhat; ◻ CIT according to the norms of income distribution, established by the regional maslikhat in the amount of not more than 50% of the received tax deductions, except for receipts from large businesses according to the list approved by the central authorized body for state planning together with the central authorized body for budget execution, and receipts from oil sector organizations; ◻ social tax according to the norms of income distribution established by the regional maslikhat; ◻ payment for negative impact on the environment; ◻ payment for the use of water resources of surface sources; ◻ payment for forest uses; ◻ fee for issuance or extension of a permit to hire foreign labor in the RK; ◻ payment for the use of plant resources in the order of special use of plant life; ◻ payment for the use of wildlife; ◻ payment for reimbursement of historical costs.	Article 28. Receipts to the regional budget 1. Tax revenues to the regional budget are: ◻ PIT according to the norms of income distribution established by the regional maslikhat; ◻ CIT according to the norms of income distribution, established by the regional maslikhat in the amount of not more than 50% of the received tax deductions, except for receipts from business entities according to the list determined and approved in accordance with subparagraph (1) of paragraph 1 of Article 26 of this Code, and receipts from organizations of the oil sector ; ◻ social tax according to the norms of income distribution established by the regional maslikhat; ◻ payment for the use of water resources of surface sources; ◻ payment for forest uses; ◻ fee for issuance or extension of a permit to hire foreign labor in the RK; ◻ payment for the use of plant resources in the order of special use of plant life; ◻ payment for the use of wildlife; ◻ payment for reimbursement of historical costs; ◻ **payment for the use of specially protected natural territories of local significance.**

continued on next page

Table *continued*

Current Provisions of the Budget Code (effective from 4 December 2008, No. 95-IV)	Draft of the New Budget Code (posted on the website of the Majilis of the Parliament of the Republic of Kazakhstan, dated 28 September 2023: https://mazhilis.parlam.kz/#/all-bill/pending-majilis)
Tax revenues to the district (cities of regional significance) budget	
Article 52. Receipts to the district (cities of regional significance) budget 1. Tax revenues to the district (cities of regional significance) budget are: □ PIT according to the norms of income distribution, established by the regional maslikhat, with the exception of PIT on income subject to self-assessment by individuals who have on the territory of the city of district significance, village, settlement located declared at the time of registration in the state revenue authority: • location – for an individual entrepreneur, private notary, private bailiff, lawyer, professional mediator; • place of residence – for other natural persons; □ CIT according to the norms of income distribution established by the regional maslikhat in the amount of not less than 50% of the received tax deductions, except for receipts from large businesses according to the list approved by the central authorized body on state planning together with the central authorized body on budget execution, and receipts from oil sector organizations; □ social tax according to the norms of income distribution established by the regional maslikhat; □ property tax on the property of individuals and legal entities, individual entrepreneurs, except for property tax on the objects of taxation of this tax, located in the territory of the city of district significance, village, settlement, rural district; □ land tax, except for land tax on residential lands from individuals and legal entities on land plots located on the territory of a city of district significance, village, settlement; □ vehicle tax, except for vehicle tax: • from individuals whose place of residence is located in the territory of a city of district significance, village or settlement;	Article 29. Receipts to the district (cities of regional significance) budget 1. Tax revenues to the district (cities of regional significance) budget are: □ PIT according to the norms of income distribution, established by the regional maslikhat, with the exception of PIT on income subject to self-assessment by individuals who have on the territory of the city of district significance, village, settlement located declared at the time of registration in the state revenue authority: • location – for an individual entrepreneur, private notary, private bailiff, lawyer, professional mediator; • place of residence – for other individuals; □ CIT according to the norms of distribution of revenues established by the regional maslikhat in the amount of not less than 50% of the received tax deductions, except for receipts from large businesses on the list determined and approved in accordance with subparagraph (1) of paragraph 1 of Article 26 of this Code, and receipts from oil sector organizations; □ social tax according to the norms of income distribution established by the regional maslikhat; □ property tax on the property of individuals and legal entities, individual entrepreneurs, except for the property tax on the objects of taxation of this tax, located in the territory of the city of district significance, village, settlement, rural district; □ land tax, except for land tax on residential lands from individuals and legal entities on land plots located on the territory of a city of district significance, village, settlement; □ vehicle tax, except for vehicle tax: • from individuals whose place of residence is located in the territory of a city of district significance, village or settlement;

continued on next page

Table *continued*

Current Provisions of the Budget Code (effective from 4 December 2008, No. 95-IV)	**Draft of the New Budget Code** (posted on the website of the Majilis of the Parliament of the Republic of Kazakhstan, dated 28 September 2023: https://mazhilis.parlam.kz/#/all-bill/pending-majilis)
• from legal entities whose location, indicated in their constituent documents, is located in the territory of a city of district significance, village or settlement;	• from legal entities whose location, indicated in their constituent documents, is located in the territory of a city of district significance, village or settlement;
□ excise taxes on:	□ excise taxes on:
• all types of alcohol produced on the territory of the Republic of Kazakhstan;	• all types of alcohol produced on the territory of the Republic of Kazakhstan;
• alcoholic beverages produced in the territory of the Republic of Kazakhstan;	• alcoholic beverages produced in the territory of the Republic of Kazakhstan;
• beer with a volume content of ethyl alcohol not exceeding 0.5%, produced on the territory of the Republic of Kazakhstan;	• beer products with a volume content of ethyl alcohol not exceeding 0.5%, produced on the territory of the Republic of Kazakhstan;
• tobacco products manufactured in the territory of the Republic of Kazakhstan;	• tobacco products manufactured in the territory of the Republic of Kazakhstan;
• passenger cars (except for cars with manual control or manual control adapter specially designed for persons with disabilities) manufactured in the territory of the Republic of Kazakhstan;	• passenger cars (except for cars with manual control or manual control adapter specially designed for persons with disabilities) manufactured in the territory of the Republic of Kazakhstan;
• gasoline (except jet fuel), diesel fuel, gasohol, benzanol, nephras, light hydrocarbon blends and ecological fuel;	• gasoline (except jet fuel), diesel fuel, gasohol, benzanol, nephras, light hydrocarbon blend and ecological fuel;
□ payment for the use of land plots, except for land plots located on the territory of a city of district significance, village, settlement;	□ payment for the use of land plots, except for land plots located on the territory of a city of district significance, village, settlement;
□ license fee for the right to engage in certain types of activity (fee for issuing licenses to engage in certain types of activity);	□ license fee for the right to engage in certain types of activities (fee for issuing licenses to engage in certain types of activities);
□ fees for the use of licenses to engage in certain types of activities;	□ fees for the use of licenses to engage in certain types of activities;
□ fee for state (accounting) registration of legal entities, their branches and representative offices, except for commercial organizations, as well as their re-registration;	□ fee for state (accounting) registration of legal entities, their branches and representative offices, except for commercial organizations, as well as their re-registration;
□ fee for state registration of vehicles, as well as their re-registration;	□ fee for state registration of vehicles, as well as their re-registration;
□ fee for state registration of pledge of movable property and vessel mortgage, as well as state registration of irrevocable authorization for deregistration and removal of the aircraft;	□ fee for state registration of pledge of movable property and vessel mortgage, as well as state registration of irrevocable authorization for deregistration and removal of the aircraft;

continued on next page

Table *continued*

Current Provisions of the Budget Code (effective from 4 December 2008, No. 95-IV)	Draft of the New Budget Code (posted on the website of the Majilis of the Parliament of the Republic of Kazakhstan, dated 28 September 2023: https://mazhilis.parlam.kz/#/all-bill/pending-majilis)
▫ payment for placement of outdoor (visual) advertising in the open space outside the premises in the city of regional significance, in the right-of-way of public highways passing through the territory of the city of regional significance; ▫ state duty, except for consular fees and state duties credited to the republican budget.	▫ payment for placement of outdoor (visual) advertising in the open space outside the premises in the city of regional significance, in the right-of-way of public highways passing through the territory of the city of regional significance; ▫ state duty, except for consular fees and state duties credited to the republican budget; ▫ **unified land tax;** ▫ **mining tax on commonly occurring minerals, underground water and therapeutic mud, except for mineral extraction tax on commonly occurring minerals, underground water and therapeutic mud located on the territory of a city of district significance, village, settlement, rural district.**
Tax revenues to the budgets of a raion city, village, settlement, rural district	
Article 52-1. Receipts to the budgets of a city of regional significance, village, settlement, rural district 1. Tax revenues to the budgets of a city of regional significance, village, settlement, rural district are: ▫ PIT on income subject to self-assessment by individuals who have a declared on the territory of a city of district significance, village, settlement located at the time of registration with the state revenue authority: • location – for an individual entrepreneur, private notary, private bailiff, lawyer, professional mediator; • place of residence – for other natural persons; ▫ personal property tax on objects subject to this tax located in the territory of a city of district significance, village, settlement, rural district; ▫ land tax on residential lands from individuals and legal entities on land plots located on the territory of a city of district significance, village, settlement; ▫ unified land tax;	Article 30. Receipts to the budgets of a city of regional significance, village, settlement, rural district 1. Tax revenues to the budgets of a city of regional significance, village, settlement, rural district are: ▫ PIT on income subject to self-assessment by individuals who have a declared on the territory of a city of district significance, village, settlement located at the time of registration with the state revenue authority: • location – for an individual entrepreneur, private notary, private bailiff, lawyer, professional mediator; • place of residence – for other natural persons; ▫ personal property tax on objects subject to this tax located in the territory of a city of district significance, village, settlement, rural district; ▫ land tax on residential lands from individuals and legal entities on land plots located on the territory of a city of district significance, village, settlement; ▫ unified land tax;

continued on next page

Table *continued*

Current Provisions of the Budget Code (effective from 4 December 2008, No. 95-IV)	**Draft of the New Budget Code** (posted on the website of the Majilis of the Parliament of the Republic of Kazakhstan, dated 28 September 2023: https://mazhilis.parlam.kz/#/all-bill/pending-majilis)
◻ vehicle tax: • from individuals whose place of residence is located in the territory of a city of district significance, village or settlement; • from legal entities whose location, indicated in their constituent documents, is located on the territory of a city of district significance, village or settlement; ◻ payment for the use of land plots; ◻ payment for the placement of outdoor (visual) advertising: • in the open space outside the premises in the city of district significance, village, settlement; • in the right-of-way of public highways passing through the territories of a city of district significance, village, settlement, rural district; • in open space outside the premises outside populated areas and outside the right-of-way of public highways.	◻ vehicle tax: • from individuals whose place of residence is located in the territory of a city of district significance, village or settlement; • from legal entities whose location, indicated in their constituent documents, is located on the territory of a city of district significance, village or settlement; ◻ payment for the use of land plots; ◻ payment for the placement of outdoor (visual) advertising: • in the open space outside the premises in the city of district significance, village, settlement; • in the right-of-way of public highways passing through the territories of a city of district significance, village, settlement, rural district; • in open space outside the premises outside populated areas and outside the right-of-way of public highways; ◻ **mining tax on commonly occurring minerals, groundwater and therapeutic mud located in the territory of a raion city, village, settlement or rural district.**

APPENDIX 5

Key Indicators of the Radio Frequency Spectrum in Kazakhstan

The **fee for the use of the radio frequency spectrum** is levied on the **nominal values** (bands, ranges) of the radio frequency spectrum allocated by the authorized state body responsible for implementing state policy in the field of communications.

Fee Payers

The fee is payable by individuals and entities that have obtained the **right to use the radio frequency spectrum**.

Exemptions

The following entities are exempt from paying the fee:

1. **State institutions** that utilize the radio frequency spectrum for the performance of their core functional duties;
2. **Television and radio broadcasting organizations** that have paid the fee associated with obtaining a permit for radio frequency spectrum use, issued by the authorized state body responsible for communications policy *(excluding state institutions that receive such permits for official functional purposes)*.
3. **Owners of radio stations in the CB-band (27 MHz)**, provided the frequencies are used for a single station.

Fee Rates

The **annual fee rates** are calculated as a multiple of the **monthly calculation index,** determined **by type of radio communication** and based on the **territory of use** of the radio frequency spectrum (**Table A5.1**).

For **digital terrestrial television and radio broadcasting**, the **fee for the use of the radio frequency spectrum** is determined based on:

- **The frequency range** allocated for broadcasting;
- **The territory of use** of the radio frequency spectrum.

The specific fee rates are outlined in **Table A5.2**.

Table A5.1: Annual Fee Rates for the Use of the Radio Frequency Sector for the Following Types of Radio Communications

No.	Type of Radio Communication	Area of Use	Fee Rate (monthly calculation index)
1.	Radio personal radio call systems (for frequency assignment of 25 kHz width)	Region, city of republican significance and capital	10
2.	Trunking communication (per 25 kHz radio channel for receiving/25 kHz for transmitting)		
2.1.		City of republican significance and capital	140
2.2.		Settlement with a population of more than 50,000 people	80
2.3.		Other administrative-territorial units (city of district significance, district, settlement, village, rural district)	10
3.	Ultrashort wave radio communication (per 25 kHz duplex channel for receiving/25 kHz for transmitting)		
3.1.		City of republican significance and capital	80
3.2.		Settlement with a population of more than 50,000 people	60
3.3.		Other administrative-territorial units (city of district significance, district, settlement, village, rural district)	15
4.	Ultrashort wave radio communication (per 25 kHz simplex channel)		
4.1.		City of republican significance and capital	30
4.2.		Settlement with a population of more than 50,000 people	20
4.3.		Other administrative-territorial units (city of district significance, district, settlement, village, rural district)	10
5.	Short wave communication (per frequency assignment) at transmitter output power	Region, city of republican significance and capital	
	– up to 50 W		10
	– over 50 W		20
6.	Radio extenders (per channel)	Region, city of republican significance and capital	2

continued on next page

Table A5.1 *continued*

No.	Type of Radio Communication	Area of Use	Fee Rate (monthly calculation index)
7.	Cellular communication (per 1 MHz bandwidth for reception/1 MHz bandwidth for transmission)	Region, city of republican significance and capital	2,300
8.	Global personal mobile satellite communications (per 100 kHz duplex bandwidth for reception/100 kHz for transmission)	Republic of Kazakhstan	20
9.	Satellite communication with HUB technology (per 100 kHz bandwidth on reception/100 kHz bandwidth on transmission used on HUB)	Republic of Kazakhstan	30
9.1.	Satellite communications using non-geostationary satellites (per 2 MHz bandwidth for reception/2 MHz bandwidth for transmission, per one receiving and transmitting device of the interfacing station)	Republic of Kazakhstan	1
10.	Satellite communication without HUB technology (for frequencies used by one station)	Republic of Kazakhstan	100
11.	Radio relay lines (per duplex trunk on one span)		
11.1.	- local	District, city, town, settlement, village, rural district	40
11.2.	- zonal and trunk	Republic of Kazakhstan	10
12.	Wireless radio access systems (per 25 kHz duplex channel for reception/25 kHz for transmission)		
12.1.		Settlement with a population of more than 50,000 people	25
12.2.		Other administrative-territorial units (city of district significance, raion, district, settlement, village, rural district)	2
13.	Wireless radio access systems using broadband signal technology (per duplex channel width of 2 MHz/2 MHz for reception and 2 MHz for transmission)		
13.1.		City of republican significance and capital	140

continued on next page

Table A5.1 *continued*

No.	Type of Radio Communication	Area of Use	Fee Rate (monthly calculation index)
13.2.		Settlement with a population of more than 50,000 people	70
13.3.		Other administrative-territorial units (city of district significance, raion, district, settlement, village, rural district)	5
14.	Terrestrial cable television (for 8 MHz frequency band)		
14.1.		Settlement with a population of more than 200,000 people	300
14.2.		Settlement with a population of 50,000 to 200,000 people	135
14.3.		City of district significance with a population of up to 50,000 people, a district	45
14.4.		Other administrative-territorial units (settlement, village, rural district)	5
15.	Maritime radio communication (radio modem, shore communication, telemetry, radar, etc.), per radio channel	Region	10

kHz = kilohertz, MHz = megahertz, W = watt.

Source: Authors' compilation based on Code of the Republic of Kazakhstan "On Taxes and other Obligatory Payments to the Budget (Tax Code)" (effective from 25 December 2017, No. 120-VI).

Table A5.2: Annual Fee Rates for the Use of the Radio Frequency Sector for Digital Terrestrial Broadcasting

No.	Frequency Range for Digital Terrestrial Television and Radio Broadcasting	Area of Use	Fee Rate (monthly calculation index)
1.	Television/meter band frequencies		
1.1.	Power of transmitting radio-electronic means up to and including 50 W	City of republican significance	81
		Region	15
1.2.	Power of transmitting radio-electronic means up to and including 250 W	City of republican significance	361
		Region	65
1.3.	Power of transmitting radio-electronic means up to and including 500 W	City of republican significance	957
		Region	174

continued on next page

Table A5.2 *continued*

No.	Frequency Range for Digital Terrestrial Television and Radio Broadcasting	Area of Use	Fee Rate (monthly calculation index)
1.4.	Power of transmitting radio-electronic means up to and including 1,000 W	City of republican significance	1,353
		Region	245
1.5.	Power of transmitting radio-electronic means over 1,000 W	City of republican significance	2,344
		Region	425
2.	Television/decimeter frequency range		
2.1.	Power of transmitting radio-electronic means up to and including 50 W	City of republican significance	51
		Region	9
2.2.	Power of transmitting radio-electronic means up to and including 250 W	City of republican significance	228
		Region	41
2.3.	Power of transmitting radio-electronic means up to and including 500 W	City of republican significance	605
		Region	110
2.4.	Power of transmitting radio-electronic means up to and including 1,000 W	City of republican significance	855
		Region	155
2.5.	Power of transmitting radio-electronic means over 1,000 W	City of republican significance	1,481
		Region	269

W = watt.

Source: Authors' compilation based on Code of the Republic of Kazakhstan "On Taxes and other Obligatory Payments to the Budget (Tax Code)" (effective from 25 December 2017, No. 120-VI).

Main Applications of the Radio Frequency Spectrum in Kazakhstan

The radio frequency spectrum in Kazakhstan is utilized across various sectors, including telecommunications, broadcasting, and industry. The primary areas of application are as follows:

- **Mobile communication.** Radio frequencies are used to provide mobile communication services (2G, 3G, 4G, 5G), including voice communication, data transmission, and mobile internet. This is one of the most dynamically expanding segments of the spectrum.
- **Radio broadcasting and television.** Frequency ranges are allocated for analogue and digital television, radio stations, and satellite communications, encompassing both terrestrial and satellite broadcasting.
- **Wireless internet and fixed communication.** Radio frequencies support wireless internet services (Wi-Fi, LTE, WiMAX) and fixed wireless connections, facilitating connectivity in remote areas.

- **Satellite communication.** Frequencies are designated for satellite-based communication, including voice transmission, data services, and internet connectivity, as well as radio navigation and meteorological systems.
- **Telecommunications networks for industry.** Radio frequencies enable the development and operation of private telecommunications networks in sectors such as industry, transport, and energy.
- **Other applications.** This category includes specialized radio frequency uses for various technological and operational needs.

Regulation and Authorization of Radio Frequency Spectrum Use

In Kazakhstan, authorization is required for the use of the radio frequency spectrum. This regulation applies to television and radio broadcasting, mobile operators, taxi services, and other industries, including the military.

The Telecommunications Committee of the Ministry of Digital Development, Innovation, and Aerospace Industry of the Republic of Kazakhstan is responsible for the distribution, allocation, and assignment of frequency bands for civilian purposes, while the Ministry of Defense oversees spectrum allocation for military needs.

Frequency values are allocated to different sectors, each with its designated range, as specified in the National Table of Frequency Band Allocation for Radio Services. This table covers the entire spectrum from 3 kHz to 400 GHz, accommodating all types of radio-electronic environments.

Types of Communication Requiring Authorization

Permission to use the radio frequency spectrum is required for the following types of communication:

- Ultrashort wave radio communication;
- Short wave communication;
- Mainline radio relay lines;
- Zone radio relay lines;
- Local radio relay lines;
- Radio relay lines for television signal transmission;
- Terrestrial satellite communication stations;
- Mobile satellite communication systems;
- Wireless Radio Access networks (Wireless Local Loop: WLL);
- Data transmission networks (ultrashort wave);
- Satellite digital television broadcasting;
- Third-generation cellular communication (3G);
- Fourth-generation mobile communication (4G);
- Over-the-air cable television;
- Television broadcasting.

Table A5.3: Key Radio Frequency Spectrum Indicators in Kazakhstan for 2023
(1,000 units)

Indicators	Actual Volume	Of Which in Rural Areas
Number of fixed telephone lines	2,686.9	729.6
Number of fixed internet subscribers	3,058.9	632.5
Number of fixed (wired) internet subscribers	2,916.5	559.8
Number of subscribers to wireless broadband internet access using satellite links	1.9	0.4
Number of subscribers of wireless broadband internet access using land fixed lines	140.5	72.3
Number of mobile subscribers	25,532.0	
Number of cable television head-end stations (systems), units	59	5
Number of cable television subscribers	481.8	4.4
Number of satellite TV subscribers	1,487.7	826.3
Number of digital interactive television (IPTV) subscribers	1,185.9	193.5

Source: Authors' compilation based on data from the Bureau of National Statistics of the Agency for Strategic Planning and Reforms of the Republic of Kazakhstan.

Telecommunications Market in Kazakhstan

Fixed-Line and Mobile Communications

As of 2023, Kazakhstan had 2.6 million fixed-line subscribers (landline phone users), with 27.2% residing in rural areas. However, the share of fixed-line communications in the overall telecommunications market continues to decline, being increasingly replaced by mobile services. This shift is driven primarily by the growing availability and flexibility of mobile technologies, which offer users a wider range of services, including mobile internet and diverse data plans.

Reflecting this trend, the number of registered mobile subscribers in Kazakhstan has exceeded 25.5 million, highlighting a strong transition toward more convenient and economically attractive solutions.

Television Market

In the television sector, subscriber distribution by service type is as follows:

- Satellite TV: 47.1%;
- Digital interactive TV: 37.6%;
- Cable TV: 15.3%.

These figures reflect growing preference for satellite and digital technologies, which offer higher image quality and ease of use. Satellite TV is particularly advantageous owing to its widespread availability, especially in regions with limited connectivity options. Meanwhile, digital interactive television attracts users with flexible services and advanced content management features, aligning with the increasing demand for high-tech solutions in the market.

Telecommunications Operators

According to the Telecommunications Committee of the Ministry of Digital Development, Innovation, and Aerospace Industry of the Republic of Kazakhstan, approximately 20 telecom operators are active in the national telecommunications market, providing long-distance and international telephone services, internet access, and satellite mobile communications. Additionally, Kazakhstan has three major mobile operators:

- Kcell JSC (operating under the Kcell and Activ trademarks);
- Kar-Tel LLP (operating under the Beeline trademark);
- Mobile Telecom-Service LLP (operating under the Tele2 and Altel trademarks).

Internet Access and Infrastructure Development

Expanding universal internet access remains a key priority in Kazakhstan's communications sector. To meet the demand for high-quality internet services, various wired and wireless technologies are currently in use, including:

- ADSL (Asymmetric Digital Subscriber Line);
- FTTN (Fiber-to-the-Node);
- 3G;
- 4G/LTE (Long-Term Evolution);
- CDMA/EVDO (Code-Division Multiple Access/Evolution-Data-Optimized).

These technologies play a crucial role in enhancing connectivity across the country, ensuring residents—in both urban and rural areas—have access to reliable and high-speed internet services.

Table A5.4: Spectrum Allocation and Availability of Radio Frequency Bands for 2023

Radio Frequency Spectrum Indicator	
Traffic of fixed (wired) broadband access to internet, gigabytes	6,803,923,179.6
Traffic of fixed wireless broadband access to internet	26,778,633.4
Mobile internet traffic, gigabytes	5,111,681,156.4
Percentage of cellular network coverage in the territory	55.0
3G network	33.0
4G network	15.8

continued on next page

Table A5.4 *continued*

Radio Frequency Spectrum Indicator	
Percentage of coverage of the territory by terrestrial digital television broadcasting	100.0
Percentage of population coverage by cellular network	98.2
3G network	95.0
4G network	89.2
5G network	38.2

Source: Authors' compilation based on data from the Bureau of National Statistics of the Agency for Strategic Planning and Reforms of the Republic of Kazakhstan.

Internet Infrastructure and Usage in Kazakhstan

Broadband Network Deployment

According to the Telecommunications Committee of the Ministry of Digital Development, Innovations, and Aerospace Industry of the Republic of Kazakhstan, the deployment of FTTH/B (Fiber-to-the-Home/Building) networks using fiber-optic connectivity has been completed in major cities, providing users with internet speeds of up to 120 Mbps.

In regional centers and major cities, broadband internet is available through ADSL technology, offering bandwidths of up to 8 Mbps, as well as 3G/4G/LTE wireless services, with a maximum data transfer rate of up to 4 Mbps. In rural areas with populations of 50 or more, internet and telephony services are provided using CDMA/EVDO and 3G technologies.

By the end of 2023, out of 6,406 localities, 116 cities and 4,858 villages had access to broadband internet via 3G and/or 4G mobile networks.

Internet Traffic Distribution

The distribution of internet traffic in Kazakhstan highlights the preferences for different types of internet access:

- Fixed (wired) internet accounts for 57% of total traffic, the largest share. Its popularity owes to the high stability and bandwidth of wired networks, making this the preferred choice for home and office users who require reliable, high-speed connections for work, video streaming, and other data-intensive online services.
- Mobile internet represents 42.8% of total traffic, reflecting the growing mobility of the population and the increasing demand for constant internet access. Mobile connectivity offers flexibility and convenience, allowing users to stay connected while on the move, aligning with the needs of a modern, dynamic lifestyle.
- Wireless internet (e.g., Wi-Fi) accounts for just 0.2% of total traffic. This limited usage is attributed to the uneven distribution of wireless communication technologies across regions, as well as their lower stability and bandwidth compared to wired and mobile networks.

Table A5.5: Key Indicators of the Radio Frequency Spectrum by Regions of Kazakhstan for 2023

Region	Population ('000s)	No. of Fixed Telephone Lines ('000s)	Of Total No. of Fixed Telephone Lines in Rural Areas ('000s)	No. of Fixed Internet Subscribers ('000s)	Traffic of Fixed (Wired) Broadband Access to Internet, GB	Traffic of Fixed Wireless Broadband Access to Internet, GB
Kazakhstan	**19,767**	**2,686.9**	**729.6**	**3,058.9**	**6,803,923,179.6**	**26,778,633.4**
Abay region	610	95.3	29.7	100.9	200,863,044.0	931,933.1
Akmola region	788	159.0	68.3	131.7	341,185,081.2	1,508,257.1
Aktobe region	928	137.0	33.0	156.2	327,335,349.3	5,513,541.9
Almaty region	1,506	158.3	121.0	142.7	426,826,612.6	5,886,624.4
Atyrau region	693	115.7	40.4	103.2	325,791,506.5	987,203.2
West Kazakhstan region	688	78.3	26.3	89.4	171,029,851.7	700,191.5
Zhambyl region	1,218	89.4	40.9	99.5	218,846,458.7	623,636.3
Zhetisu region	699	80.6	30.4	87.7	176,786,673.9	653,238.5
Karaganda region	1,135	200.9	34.6	235.4	360,002,639.0	1,038,741.5
Kostanay region	832	174.7	61.6	189.3	381,368,849.5	1,064,188.7
Kyzylorda region	834	76.0	35.7	81.6	196,886,600.3	529,199.4
Mangystau region	767	64.2	13.9	124.1	255,111,769.3	275,021.1
Pavlodar region	755	144.5	34.6	177.4	340,060,640.1	1,599,154.6
North Kazakhstan region	534	124.1	62.1	116.9	217,515,740.0	823,084.6
Turkestan region	2,119	82.0	52.9	72.2	175,013,807.0	1,180,612.0
Ulytau region	221	29.4	6.8	44.3	49,153,107.5	247,986.9
East Kazakhstan region	730	143.0	37.2	143.9	282,592,232.6	1,175,931.1
Astana	1,355	226.1	0.3	365.8	1,007,895,757.9	369,159.1
Almaty	2,162	441.6	–	490.1	1,145,630,897.9	1,226,433.9
Shymkent	1,192	66.8	–	106.5	204,026,560.6	444,494.5

Source: Authors' compilation based on data from the Bureau of National Statistics of the Agency for Strategic Planning and Reforms of the Republic of Kazakhstan.

Telecommunications Coverage and Digital Accessibility in Kazakhstan

Current State of Telecommunications Coverage

In 2023, the level of fixed-line telephone coverage and the availability of wired and wireless internet (excluding mobile communications) reached approximately 29.1% of the total population. This figure reflects the early stage of digital accessibility in Kazakhstan, where only about 30% of the population has access to basic telecommunications services. However, achieving full-scale digital progress requires continued expansion of coverage and closing the digital divide between regions.

Regional Disparities in Telecommunications Infrastructure

A high level of communication and internet availability is observed in major cities, including Astana (43.7%) and Almaty (43.1%). This owes largely to the development of telecommunications infrastructure, including:

- Broadband internet based on fiber-optic networks;
- Extensive mobile network coverage;
- Widespread deployment of Wi-Fi in public places, offices, and commercial centers.

These factors contribute to improving quality of life, stimulating business development, and accelerating digitalization in key economic sectors, making these cities more competitive and attractive for investment.

In contrast, Turkestan region, despite having a high population density (2.1 million people), has low communication coverage (7.3%). This highlights unequal distribution of telecommunications resources, limiting access to key economic opportunities such as remote work, e-commerce, and online education. Poor communication infrastructure reduces business competitiveness, hinders economic diversification, and makes it more difficult to attract investment into underdeveloped industries.

Regions with low connectivity remain isolated from national and global markets, restricting entrepreneurship, job creation, and innovation. Addressing this challenge requires strategic investments in telecommunications infrastructure, enabling these regions to be fully integrated into Kazakhstan's digital and economic ecosystem.

Market Trends and Increasing Internet Adoption

An analysis of market trends indicates a growing shift from traditional landline telephony to modern internet services:

- Wired and wireless internet penetration has reached 15.5%.
- Fixed-line telephone coverage remains lower, at 13.6%.

This trend reflects a clear user preference for more flexible and functional communication solutions, driven by increasing demand for high-speed data transfer and digital services.

The steady rise in internet traffic is fueled by:

- The expansion of the digital economy;
- Growing consumption of entertainment content;
- The business sector's transition to digital platforms.

These developments highlight the central role of digital technologies in economic growth and underscore the increasing demand for affordable, high-speed internet, which is essential for both individuals and businesses in a rapidly digitalizing and globalizing environment.

Government Investments in Telecommunications Infrastructure

Public spending on telecommunications infrastructure in Kazakhstan focuses on:

- Modernizing and expanding communication networks;
- Improving access to internet services;
- Enhancing connectivity in remote and rural areas.

These investments are partially integrated into state programs, including the National Infrastructure Plan of the Republic of Kazakhstan until 2029.

The plan outlines critical projects (List A), which are designated as high-priority digital transformation initiatives for Kazakhstan's telecommunications infrastructure. These projects are implemented by the Ministry of Digital Development, Innovation, and Aerospace Industry of the Republic of Kazakhstan in coordination with local authorities (*akimats* of regions and the cities of Astana, Almaty, and Shymkent).

Additionally, the plan includes projects under List B, which are scheduled for implementation depending on favorable financing conditions. The program also defines target indicators for domestic value creation, ensuring that local expertise and resources are utilized in infrastructure development.

Table A5.6: Financial Support for the Digital Transformation of Telecommunications Infrastructure Until 2029 (T1,000)

Project Name	Realization Period	Amount of Financing	Sources of Funding		
			Republican Budget	Local Budget	Extrabudgetary Funds
Construction of digital infrastructure (fiber-optic communication line [FOCL]) and installation of automated mechanized systems, transmission, and power supply to cover mobile broadband data transmission of republican and main region roads	2024–2027	61,000,000	54,900,000	**6,100,000**	0
Providing network data carrier (NDC) to a population of more than 250 people with access to mobile internet via 4G technology	2024–2027	100,104,000	0	0	100,104,000
Implementation of the project "Provision of Broadband NDC Data Transmission via FOCL"	2024–2027	532,109,020	73,600,020	0	458,509,000
Provision of republican and main region roads with mobile broadband access networks using digital infrastructure	2024–2027	30,000,000	0	0	30,000,000
Total expenditures (List A)		**723,213,020**	**128,500,020**	**6,100,000**	**588,613,000**
Construction of FOCL for households under the project Subsidizing "Last Mile" Internet to Households in NDC	2024–2027	46,000,000	0	0	46,000,000
Organization of satellite channels to sparsely populated rural areas using space communications system resources to provide broadband services	2023–2027	9,964,488	9,964,488	0	0
Establishment of a data processing center (DPC) for government agencies with hot and cold backups	2024–2025	37,000,000	37,000,000	0	0
Construction of a new DPC in Astana city, DPC Kazakhtelecom JSC	2024–2025	15,000,000		0	15,000,000
Total expenditures (List B)		**107,964,488**	**46,964,488**	**0**	**61,000,000**

Source: Authors' compilation based on the National Infrastructure Plan 2029.

As part of the digital transformation of telecommunications infrastructure, the following priority strategic tasks and target indicators are planned for implementation by 2029.

Table A5.7: Objectives and Target Indicators for the Digital Transformation of Telecommunications Infrastructure Until 2029 (%)

Objective/Target Indicator	2024	2025	2026	2027	2028	2029
Broadband internet access coverage	80	85	90	100	–	–
Bringing fiber-optic communication lines to villages	50	60	80	90	100	–
Share of provision of republican and main region roads with mobile internet using digital infrastructure	50	60	70	80	90	100
Construction of alternative direct channel Europe–East Asia	10	100	–	–	–	–
Share of transit data processed locally of total Asia–Europe traffic	2	2.50	5	5.50	6	6

Source: Authors' compilation based on the National Infrastructure Plan 2029.

Fiscal Decentralization and the Development of Telecommunications Infrastructure

Opportunities for Local Authorities Through Fiscal Decentralization

Fiscal decentralization, particularly the transfer of tax revenues from fees for the use of the radio frequency spectrum from the national budget to local budgets, presents new opportunities for local authorities to finance projects that drive the digital transformation of telecommunications infrastructure. This can lead to improved communication quality, expanded digital services, and economic growth at the regional level. Enhanced telecommunications infrastructure can stimulate employment growth, increase investment attractiveness, and support the development of new technology industries.

To increase tax revenues via use of the radio frequency spectrum, local authorities can implement strategies aimed at optimizing spectrum use and strengthening state control.

Optimizing Radio Frequency Spectrum Use for Increased Revenue

One key measure is to delegate regulatory authority to local governments, allowing them to adjust (increase) fee rates based on the economic characteristics of the region. These adjustments should consider factors such as:

- The need to develop telecommunications infrastructure;
- Attracting investment;
- Supporting innovative technologies.

An increase in spectrum fees for commercial telecom operators could provide an additional revenue stream for local budgets. However, to ensure balanced and effective implementation, a comprehensive market analysis is necessary to prevent negative impacts on competition and service affordability. If executed properly, raising fees would not only boost tax revenues but also promote more efficient use of radio frequency resources, thereby attracting further investment in telecommunications infrastructure.

Enhancing Control Over Illegal Spectrum Use

Allocating radio frequency spectrum revenues to local budgets would create stronger incentives for local authorities to monitor and prevent illegal spectrum use. By identifying and addressing violations, local governments could minimize financial losses caused by unauthorized broadcasts and illegal equipment installations. The introduction of effective monitoring and enforcement systems would promote:

- Fairer spectrum distribution;
- A more transparent and competitive market;
- Increased budget revenues.

However, implementing efficient control mechanisms would require additional funding to develop and maintain enforcement infrastructure.

Encouraging Investment in Telecommunications Infrastructure

Local governments can also stimulate investment in telecommunications infrastructure by:

- Developing incentive programs for telecom companies;
- Providing tax reductions or exemptions to encourage sector growth.

Such measures would accelerate network expansion and increase spectrum usage, ultimately leading to higher tax revenues from increased coverage and usage intensity. In addition, these initiatives would create new jobs and enhance service quality. Although such policies require short-term financial investments, the long-term economic benefits—including sustainable sector growth and increased revenues—would far outweigh the initial costs.

Streamlining Infrastructure Development Procedures

Facilitating the approval process for telecommunications infrastructure projects could accelerate the deployment of:

- Base stations;
- Network expansion initiatives;
- Other communication infrastructure.

This would lead to more efficient spectrum utilization, expanded coverage, and higher tax revenues from telecom operators. However, a balanced approach is necessary to avoid market oversaturation and infrastructure overload, ensuring stable and sustainable sector growth.

Promoting 5G Adoption and Regional Economic Growth

Supporting the deployment of 5G technology could serve as a key driver of tax revenue growth from spectrum usage while also stimulating job creation. The economic benefits of 5G implementation include:

- Increased productivity;
- Greater investment inflows into the region;
- Accelerated economic growth.

However, significant capital investment and time are required to develop the necessary 5G infrastructure, making careful planning essential.

Long-Term Impact of Fiscal Decentralization in Telecommunications

The transfer of tax revenues from radio frequency spectrum fees to local budgets, combined with proactive local government strategies, presents significant opportunities for:

- Developing digital infrastructure;
- Enhancing economic growth at the regional level;
- Boosting tax revenues through optimized spectrum use.

By adjusting fee rates, strengthening enforcement against illegal spectrum use, and incentivizing investment, local governments can improve communication services, increase employment, and attract investment.

Additionally, promoting new technologies such as 5G, simplifying permit procedures for infrastructure development, and introducing tax incentives will ensure the sustainable growth of the telecommunications sector. However, a balanced approach is necessary to:

- Prevent excessive market concentration;
- Avoid infrastructure strain;
- Minimize negative impacts on competition and service accessibility.

A comprehensive implementation of these measures will significantly increase the economic attractiveness of Kazakhstan's regions, accelerate digital transformation, and establish a sustainable telecommunications infrastructure capable of supporting long-term economic growth and development.

APPENDIX 6

Key Indicators of Digital Mining in Kazakhstan

Digital Mining Fee

The digital mining fee is levied based on the amount of electrical energy consumed during digital mining operations.

Payers of the Digital Mining Fee

The fee is payable by:

- Individuals and entities engaged in digital mining within the territory of Kazakhstan;
- Service providers offering computing infrastructure for digital mining operations, including data processing and computational services.

Fee Calculation Rates

Digital mining fees are calculated as follows:

- T2 per kilowatt-hour of electricity consumed during the reporting period;
- T1 per kilowatt-hour when using electricity generated from renewable energy sources at private power plants within Kazakhstan or from independent generating units not connected to the Unified Electric Power System of the Republic of Kazakhstan.

Regulatory Framework for Digital Mining

To establish a favorable regulatory environment for the development of the digital ecosystem, including blockchain technologies and the crypto industry, the Law of the Republic of Kazakhstan "On Digital Assets" was signed on 6 February 2023 and entered into force on 1 April 2023. This law represents a significant step toward integrating digital mining into the national economy while ensuring stability and transparency in this rapidly growing sector.

Under this legislation, the Government of Kazakhstan has introduced several key regulatory measures:

1. Mandatory Registration of Digital Miners

- All entities engaged in digital mining are required to register as individual entrepreneurs or legal entities.
- This ensures the legalization of mining activities, facilitating smoother interaction with government agencies and tax authorities.

2. Licensing of Mining Activities

Two categories of digital mining activities have been established:

- Miners with their own infrastructure. These are data processing center owners who manage and operate their own mining equipment.

- Miners renting capacity. These are equipment owners who lease server capacity in data centers. They are not subject to energy quota applications, simplifying regulation and reducing strain on the national power system.

3. Creation of a Registry for Hardware and Software Systems

- A registry of hardware and software systems has been introduced to enhance control over the mining equipment in use.
- This measure allows law enforcement agencies to identify contraband or illegally purchased equipment, protecting the economy from illicit activities and improving market transparency.

4. Cryptocurrency Production Monitoring

- A state monitoring mechanism has been implemented to track and regulate the volume of cryptocurrencies mined.
- Digital miners are legally required to operate exclusively through accredited mining pools registered in Kazakhstan.
- This enhances government oversight of mining activities and reduces risks associated with unauthorized transactions.

Introduction of the Digital Mining Fee as a Fiscal Regulatory Tool

The digital mining fee, introduced under the Tax Code, became effective on 1 January 2022 as an initial step toward the fiscal regulation and oversight of the rapidly expanding sector. It provided:

- Immediate budget revenues from mining operations;
- Basic regulatory control over mining activities prior to the introduction of comprehensive sector-specific legislation.

The introduction of mining fees also contributed to:

- The establishment of a structured tax framework, ensuring financial stability and predictability within the digital asset sector;
- Improved transparency and regulatory oversight, allowing authorities to monitor mining activities effectively.

Thus, the implementation of digital mining fees under the Tax Code served as an interim regulatory measure, paving the way for a fully legal and structured digital mining industry. This step not only generated initial state revenues but also laid the foundation for further regulatory development, increasing investor confidence and enhancing Kazakhstan's competitiveness in the global digital asset market.

Licensing of Digital Mining Activities

As of 8 January 2025, the Ministry of Digital Development, Innovation, and Aerospace Industry of the Republic of Kazakhstan has issued 24 licenses under the first category, covering digital miners who own or have legal rights to operate digital mining data processing centers (Table A6.1).

Table A6.1: Organizations with Subtype I Licenses for Digital Mining Activities

No.	Name of Digital Miner	Legal Address	Contacts
1.	AISolutions LLP	Republic of Kazakhstan, Astana, Saryarka district, Saryarka Avenue, Building 6	contact.kaz@genesisda.com
2.	Aktobe Smart Tech LLP	Republic of Kazakhstan, Aktobe region, Aktobe C.A., Aktobe city, Astana district, Aliya Moldagulova Avenue, Building 46, 303	ali-tas@bk.ru
3.	BCD Company LLP	Republic of Kazakhstan, Astana, Saryarka district, Saryarka Avenue, Building 6	contact.kaz@genesisda.com
4.	KZ Systems LLP	Republic of Kazakhstan, Astana, Saryarka district, Saryarka Avenue, Building 6	contact.kaz@genesisda.com
5.	Techno Kar LLP	Republic of Kazakhstan, Karaganda region, Karaganda C.A., Karaganda C.A., district named after Kazybek bi, Republic Avenue, House 42, Apartment 66	maratbest123@mail.ru
6.	Smart Lab Ltd	Republic of Kazakhstan, Astana, "Nura" district, Kabanbay Batyr Avenue, Building 21	smartlabkzltd@gmail.com
7.	Altyn BlockChain Co. Ltd	Republic of Kazakhstan, Astana, Esil district, Dinmuhamed Konaev Street, Building 12/1	3389240@qq.com
8.	Zhetisu Technology Co., Ltd	Republic of Kazakhstan, Astana, district "Yesil," Mangilik El Avenue, Building 55/22	frank_wind@163.com
9.	Panda Power Ltd	Republic of Kazakhstan, Astana, Esil district, Mangilik El Avenue, Building 55/22	inartva@mail.ru
10.	Netlogic Ltd	Astana, Kabanbai Batyr Avenue, 21	netlogic.bit@gmail.com
11.	Algorithm Ltd	Astana, Kabanbai Batyr Avenue, 21	algorithmltd2020@gmail.com
12.	VerCom LLP	Republic of Kazakhstan, Pavlodar region, Ekibastuz C.A., Ekibastuz city, Accounting quarter 54, Building 19	a.zhussupov@enegix.net
13.	Aqtobe Wind Energy LLP	Republic of Kazakhstan, Almaty, Medeu district, Luganskogo street, House 34, Apartment 1	aqtobewindenergy@yandex.kz
14.	Bit-Q LLP	Republic of Kazakhstan, Astana, Esil district, Dinmuhamed Konaev Street, Building 14/3	agaidarov_bm@mail.ru
15.	AGRO ENERGY LLP	Republic of Kazakhstan, Astana, Esil district, Dostyk Street, House No. 1A, Apartment 123	llyagro2019@gmail.com

continued on next page

Table A6.1 *continued*

No.	Name of Digital Miner	Legal Address	Contacts
16.	BTC KZ LLP	Republic of Kazakhstan, Almaty city, Bostandyk district, Abish Kekilbayuly Street, Building 34, 3-05	info@btc.kz
17.	Starlink Technology Ltd	Republic of Kazakhstan, Astana city, Esil district, Alikhan Bockeyhan, House 38	starlink09.23@mail.ru
18.	Digital Solutions & Co. LLP	Republic of Kazakhstan, Aktobe region, Aktobe C.A., Aktobe city, Astana district, Aliya Moldagulova Avenue, 30B, Non-Residential Premise 15a	digital-kz-kz@gmail.com
19.	Prime Data Center LLP	Republic of Kazakhstan, Aktobe region, Aktobe C.A., Aktobe city, Astana district, microdistrict 12, House 42, Apartment 27	rakhimzhanovsultan@gmail.com
20.	Azimut Capital Limited LLP	Republic of Kazakhstan, West-Kazakhstan region, Uralsk city, Sarayshyk Street 28	nabidollin@gmail.com
21.	Gas energy solution LLP	Republic of Kazakhstan, Pavlodar region, Ekibastuz C.A., Ekibastuz city, Accounting Quarter 54, Building 19	info.gasenergysolution@mail.ru
22.	Aizere KZ LLP	Republic of Kazakhstan, Almaty, Medeusky district, Manaeva Street, House 75	EIVISA2024@yandex.kz
23.	Qazmin Aqtobe LLP	Almaty city, Medeu district, Dostyk Avenue, House 132/1	jhfglfh@mail.ru
24.	Qazaq DCS LLP	Republic of Kazakhstan, Zhetisu region, Tekeli city, Tekeli city, Kunshygys Street, Building 132A	qazaqdcs@mail.ru

Source: Authors' compilation based on data from the Ministry of Digital Development, Innovation, and Aerospace Industry of the Republic of Kazakhstan.

Additionally, as of 8 January 2025, the Ministry of Digital Development, Innovation, and Aerospace Industry of the Republic of Kazakhstan has issued 29 licenses under the second category, covering digital miners who do not own or have legal rights to a digital mining data processing center but conduct mining operations using hardware and software systems they own, which are hosted within a licensed digital mining data processing center (Table A6.2).

According to the Bureau of National Statistics of the Agency for Strategic Planning and Reforms of the Republic of Kazakhstan, the industrial sector accounted for the largest share (54.9%) of total final energy consumption in 2023. The residential sector and the commercial and utility services sector were the second-largest consumers, each representing 19.0% of total energy use. The transport sector recorded the smallest share, contributing 4.2% to total energy consumption in 2023.

Table A6.2: List of Organizations with Subtype II Licenses for Digital Mining Activities

No.	Name of Digital Miner	Legal Address	Contacts
1.	KINUR INVEST TOO	Republic of Kazakhstan, Zhambyl region, Taraz C.A., Taraz city, Prospect Tole bi, Building 93A	jfoo_kinur21@mail.ru
2.	Nova Element LLP	Republic of Kazakhstan, Almaty, Bostandyk district, Gagarin Avenue, House 258B, 410	contacts@novaelement.net
3.	VerCom LLP	Republic of Kazakhstan, Pavlodar region, Ekibastuz C.A., Ekibastuz city, Accounting Quarter 54, Building 19	a.zhussupov@enegix.net
4.	LGHSTR LLP	Republic of Kazakhstan, Astana, Esil district, Dostyk Street, Building 5, Non-Residential Premise 199	lghstrllp@inbox.ru
5.	SM Digital Ltd	Republic of Kazakhstan, Astana, Esil district, Mangilik El Avenue, House 37/1, Apartment 32	kh_l@mail.ru
6.	KZ Systems LLP	Republic of Kazakhstan, Astana, Saryarka district, Saryarka Avenue, Building 6	contact.kaz@genesisda.com
7.	AISolutions LLP	Republic of Kazakhstan, Astana, Saryarka district, Saryarka Avenue, Building 6	contact.kaz@genesisda.com
8.	BCD Company LLP	Republic of Kazakhstan, Astana, Saryarka district, Saryarka Avenue, Building 6	contact.kaz@genesisda.com
9.	Infoprogservice LLP	Republic of Kazakhstan, Zhambyl region, Taraz C.A., Taraz city, Saltanat Microdistrict, House 19A	slava.rrrxxx@mail.ru
10.	Invescore Astana Ltd	Republic of Kazakhstan, Astana city, Esil district, Turkistan street, Building 16, Non-Residential Premise 56	karassaeva.a@gmail.com
11.	Canaan Creative Kazakhstan Limited Private Company	Republic of Kazakhstan, Astana, Esil district, Mangilik El Avenue, Building 55/21	moli@canaan-creative.com
12.	Silk Way Date Center Co. Ltd	Republic of Kazakhstan, Astana, Esil district, Dinmuhamed Konaev Street, Building 12/1	bitsilk.zhetisu@mail.ru
13.	JJboom Technology Ltd	Republic of Kazakhstan, Astana city, Esil district, Ulitsa Alikhan Bockeyhan, House 38, Non-Residential Premise 13	samat.karmys@gmail.com
14.	WinWay Global Ltd	Republic of Kazakhstan, Astana city, Esil district, Tyrkistan Street, Building 16, Non-Residential Premise 56	aigul@odc.kz
15.	Infobyte LLP	Republic of Kazakhstan, Almaty city, Nauryzbay district, Kalkaman-2 microdistrict, Baiken Ashimov Street, House s211	web@kazinfoteh.kz
16.	Private Company "Bitmain Kazakhstan Limited"	Republic of Kazakhstan, Astana, Esil district, Dostyk Street, 5, Non-Residential Premise 199	bt31102023@mail.ru

continued on next page

Table A6.2 *continued*

No.	Name of Digital Miner	Legal Address	Contacts
17.	NBTC KZ LLP	Republic of Kazakhstan, Almaty city, Bostandyk district, Al-Farabi Avenue, House 17	sanzhar.a@unicaselaw.com
18.	Digital Performance Group LLP	Republic of Kazakhstan, Pavlodar region, Ekibastuz C.A., Ekibastuz city, Accounting Quarter 54, Building 19	Digitalperformancegroup@mail.ru
19.	Grey Cattle Management Ltd	Republic of Kazakhstan, Astana, Esil district, Turan Street, Building 50/3	yerzattursyn@icloud.com
20.	Netlogic Ltd Private Company	Astana, Kabanbai Batyr Avenue, 21	netlogic.bit@gmail.com
21.	SmartT LLP	Republic of Kazakhstan, Zhetisu region, Taldykorgan C.A., Taldykorgan city, Abylai Khan Street, House 266	info@smart-t.kz
22.	BTMC Ltd	Republic of Kazakhstan, Astana, Esil district, Sauran Street, Building 46	Yerbolat_udeshov@mail.ru
23.	DTA Ltd	Republic of Kazakhstan, Astana city, Esil district, Dostyk Street, House 5, Non-Residential Premise 199	aki.liu@wise.sg
24.	West Smart Trading LLP	Republic of Kazakhstan, Astana city, Esil district, Sygaanak Street, Building 43, Non-Residential Premise 15	salzhanov.a.a.@mail.ru
25.	Private Company "Armada Technologies Kazakhstan Limited"	Republic of Kazakhstan, Astana, Turkistan Street, Building 16, 56	ayerishova@cbspartners.kz
26.	Joint Enterprise KAZLAT LLP	Republic of Kazakhstan, Aktobe region, Aktobe city, Astana district, Aliya Moldagulova Avenue, House 30B, Non-Residential Premise 15a	spkazlat@mail.ru
27.	Bio Synergy co LLP	Republic of Kazakhstan, Pavlodar region, Pavlodar C.A., Pavlodar city, Industrial Zone Central, Building 1940	altairastana95@gmail.com
28.	TKM EAST LLP	Republic of Kazakhstan, Almaty city, Bostandyk district, Zhandosova Street, House 34a/147, 281	a.onoprienko.asm.graf@gmail.com
29.	Friday Ventures LLP	Republic of Kazakhstan, Aktobe region, Aktobe city, Aktobe city, Astana district, C. Zhubanova Street, House 2M	fridayventures@mail.ru

Source: Authors' compilation based on data from the Ministry of Digital Development, Innovation, and Aerospace Industry of the Republic of Kazakhstan.

Table A6.3: Final Energy Consumption by Economic Sector, 2023
(million kWh)

Economic Sector	Electricity Consumption
Total energy consumption	**75,850.3**
Industry sector	**41,668.8**
Ferrous metallurgy	14,003.2
Chemical industry	2,995.7
Nonferrous metallurgy	12,592.0
Production of non-metallic products	1,996.8
Transportation equipment	54.9
Mechanical engineering	625.6
Mining industry	6,293.8
Manufacture of food, beverages, and tobacco products	1,537.5
Pulp and paper production and polygraphy	121.7
Wood industry	18.2
Construction	1,133.5
Textile and leather industry	96.2
Not elsewhere specified (industry)	199.8
Transportation sector	**3,192.0**
Domestic air transportation	–
Road transportation	53.1
Railroad transportation	2,509.8
Inland water transportation	–
Pipeline transportation	629.2
Other consumption (transportation)	–
Other sectors	**30,989.4**
Commercial and utilities	14,699.2
Housing sector (population)	14,875.7
Agriculture/forestry	1,395.8
Fishing	18.7
Not listed in other categories (other sectors)	–

kWh = kilowatt-hour.

Source: Authors' compilation based on data from the Bureau of National Statistics of the Agency for Strategic Planning and Reforms of the Republic of Kazakhstan.

In the final energy consumption structure of the industrial sector in 2023, the largest share is attributed to ferrous metallurgy (33.6%), followed by nonferrous metallurgy (30.2%) and mining (15.1%). The smallest share is recorded in the woodworking industry, accounting for 0.04% of the sector's total final consumption.

Table A6.4: Industrial Production in the Electricity Supply Sector by Region, 2023
(million kWh)

Region	Production Volume
Kazakhstan	113,585.5
Abay region	2,110.9
Akmola region	1,869.6
Aktobe region	4,344.0
Almaty region	3,506.5
Atyrau region	7,334.7
West Kazakhstan region	2,252.4
Zhambyl region	4,356.5
Zhetisu region	840.3
Karaganda region	12,229.3
Kostanay region	1,087.1
Kyzylorda region	1,646.7
Mangystau region	5,050.8
South Kazakhstan region	–
Pavlodar region	48,324.7
North Kazakhstan region	2,328.8
Turkestan region	1
Ulytau region	925.2
East Kazakhstan region	6,314.6
Astana	3,990.7
Almaty	3,172.1
Shymkent	896.2

kWh = kilowatt-hour.

Source: Authors' compilation based on data from the Bureau of National Statistics of the Agency for Strategic Planning and Reforms of the Republic of Kazakhstan.

In terms of industrial electricity production, the largest share in 2023 was generated in Pavlodar region (42.5%), followed by Karaganda region (10.8%). The smallest shares are recorded in Zhetisu region (0.7%), Ulytau region (0.8%), Shymkent city (0.8%), and Turkestan region (0.9%).

Table A6.5: Production Volume by Energy Consumption Sector, 2023
(million kWh)

Energy Consumption Sector	Production volume
Powerplants (thermal power station) (core activities)	17,965.8
Powerplants (thermal power station) (secondary activity)	8,770.7
Combined heat and power plants (core activities)	82,882.8
Combined heat and power plants (secondary activity)	3,966.2
Conversion sector – output (conversion into other fuels and energy), total	**113,585.5**

kWh = kilowatt-hour.

Source: Authors' compilation based on data from the Bureau of National Statistics of the Agency for Strategic Planning and Reforms of the Republic of Kazakhstan.

In the conversion sector, thermal energy accounts for the largest share of energy consumption, at 76.5%, while electric energy represents the smallest share, at 23.5%.

Kazakhstan's energy infrastructure development priorities until 2029 focus on ensuring energy security and achieving carbon neutrality through investment in infrastructure modernization and expansion, as well as the implementation of measures to improve energy efficiency across the economy.

The modernization of energy infrastructure aims to reduce the deterioration of generating capacities and electrical networks while upgrading equipment with modern metering systems to 100%. This will help reduce overall energy losses and the frequency of power system failures.

For example, in 2023, 56% of power plants were more than 30 years old, and the average wear and tear of power grids reached 74%. These factors, combined with an increase in power system failures, contribute to significant energy distribution losses, which currently stand at 14%.

The National Infrastructure Plan of Kazakhstan until 2029 includes projects to introduce new capacities to meet the country's growing electricity demand through extra-budgetary funding.

Projects involving the construction of new powerplants and the modernization of existing ones are classified under List A for the following reasons:

- Ensure a reliable electricity supply to the population;
- Support the operation of vital facilities;
- Serve as a key element in economic development;
- Reduce dependence on imported energy, thereby strengthening energy security;
- Lower the risk of power system failures.

Table A6.6: Financial Support to the Development of Energy Infrastructure Until 2029
(T1,000)

Project Name	Realization Period	Amount of Funding
SDPP-1 (State District Power Plant 1) with a capacity of 500 MW, a large combined heat and power plant that generates and supplies electricity and heat for the needs of the region	2012–2024	169,000,000
SDPP-2 with a capacity of 1,080 MW, one of the largest thermal power plants in Kazakhstan, playing an important role in ensuring energy supply and maintaining the stability of the country's energy system	2009–2029	–
SDPP-3 with a capacity of 1,200 MW, one of the largest thermal power plants in Kazakhstan, playing an important role in providing electricity to large industrial regions and residential areas	2024–2029	720,000,000
Aksu SDPP plans to construct unit 7 with a capacity of 325 MW, which will significantly increase its overall capacity and ability to provide reliable power supply for the region	2023–2028	340,000,000
Semipalatinsk hydropower station with a capacity of 300 MW will be built to increase electricity production through the use of water resources	2024–2029	420,000,000
SDPP Topar LLP is a thermal power plant that plans to replace the outdated 130 MW turbine unit 3, aimed at modernizing the power equipment of the plant to improve its efficiency and reliability	2021–2024	10,713,000
SDPP Topar LLP (replacement of obsolete turbine unit. 4–130 MW)	2022–2025	15,000,000
Masdar wind power plants—1 GW—to build large wind farms aimed at generating clean and sustainable energy using renewable sources	2025–2029	736,000,000
Masdar wind power plants—1 GW	2025–2029	720,000,000
TotalEnergies 1GW wind farms, building large wind farms to produce clean energy	2025–2029	515,411,430
People's Republic of China power wind powerplants—1 GW	2025–2029	562,000,000
Unification of the energy system of western Kazakhstan with the Unified Electric power system of the Republic of Kazakhstan	2021–2028	201,613,202
Strengthening of the power grid of the southern zone of the Unified Electric power system of the Republic of Kazakhstan	2021–2027	153,992,610
Strengthening of external power supply scheme of Astana city (Astana 500 kV substation and 500 kV overhead lines)	2024–2029	40,000,000
Construction of a direct current line "North–South"	2024–2029	601,440,000

GW = gigawatt, MW = megawatt, SDPP = State District Power Plant.
Source: Authors' compilation based on National Infrastructure Plan 2029.

Implementation of these measures for the development of energy infrastructure until 2029 includes the following key tasks and target indicators.

Table A6.7: Objectives and Target Indicators for the Development of Energy Infrastructure Until 2029

Objective/Target Indicator	2024	2025	2026	2027	2028	2029
Decrease in depreciation of generating capacities by 2029 to 47%	53%	50%	49%	49%	48%	47%
Share of electricity from renewable energy by 2029 12.5% of total production	6%	6,10%	7%	8%	10%	13%
Electricity capacity input with accumulation 14.785 GW by 2029	0.695 GW	0.945 GW	3.595 GW	4.725 GW	6.075 GW	14,785 GW

GW = gigawatt.

Source: Authors' compilation based on National Infrastructure Plan 2029.

Fiscal Decentralization and Energy Infrastructure Development

Fiscal decentralization, specifically the transfer of digital mining fee revenues from the national level to local budgets and the delegation of regulatory powers to local authorities (including the ability to adjust fee rates based on regional economic conditions), will create new financial opportunities for key energy infrastructure projects.

Through this process, local governments will have the flexibility to implement strategies and programs aimed at increasing digital mining profitability, ensuring sustainable financing for critical infrastructure modernization and development initiatives.

Encouraging Renewable Energy Investment

Local authorities can promote the adoption of renewable energy technologies by offering tax incentives to companies operating in this sector. This approach would:

- Attract private investment, accelerating energy infrastructure development;
- Create new jobs, improving employment rates and household incomes;
- Enhance regional economic performance, strengthening overall growth.

Upgrading the Power Grid and Smart Technologies

Revenues from digital mining fees could be allocated towards modernizing the power grid, including the introduction of smart grid technologies. These improvements would:

- Enhance energy efficiency and reduce power losses;
- Ensure a stable electricity supply, particularly during peak demand periods;
- Create a more attractive business environment, fostering investment and economic expansion.

Expanding Energy Generation and Infrastructure Modernization

With the rising electricity demand from digital mining and other industries, investing in generation capacity expansion and infrastructure modernization will help:

- Prevent future energy shortages by ensuring stable supply;
- Increase energy market predictability, a key factor in attracting investors;
- Support long-term economic growth through a reliable energy framework.

Economic and Social Benefits of Energy Modernization

The development of renewable energy sources and power grid modernization will provide additional revenue streams for local budgets. These initiatives will also:

- Require a skilled workforce, reducing unemployment and improving social conditions;
- Increase tax revenues, as business expansion and industrial production grow.

Addressing Initial Investment Challenges

Although these projects require significant capital investment in the early stages, leading to short-term financial strain on local budgets, their long-term benefits far outweigh the costs. These include:

- Lower energy costs and improved environmental conditions;
- Greater energy independence, reducing reliance on external energy sources;
- Sustained economic growth, job creation, and increased local revenues.

By leveraging fiscal decentralization and strategic investment in energy infrastructure, Kazakhstan's regions can achieve sustainable economic growth, improved energy security, and enhanced quality of life. These efforts will create jobs, boost local tax revenues, and support the long-term development of both traditional and renewable energy sectors.

REFERENCES

D. Allain-Dupré, I. Chatry, and A. Moisio. 2020. Asymmetric Decentralisation: Trends, Challenges and Policy Implications. *Regional Development Paper 10*. Organisation for Economic Co-operation and Development.

Y. Altunbaş and J. Thornton. 2012. Fiscal Decentralization and Governance. *Public Finance Review*. 40 (1). pp. 66–85.

Asian Development Bank (ADB). 2018. *Kazakhstan: Accelerating Economic Diversification*. ADB.

———. 2024. *Kazakhstan's Resource Economy Diversification Through Global Value Chains*. ADB.

J. Assunção and R. Rocha. 2016. Rural Settlements and Deforestation in the Amazon. *Working Paper*. Climate Policy Initiative.

E. Baier, H. Kroll, and A. Zenker. 2013. Templates of Smart Specialisation: Experiences of Place-Based Regional Development Strategies in Germany and Austria. *Working Paper R5/2013*. Karlsruhe: Fraunhofer Institute for Systems.

C. Baretti, B. Huber, and K. Lichtblau. 2002. A Tax on Tax Revenue: The Incentive Effects of Equalizing Transfers: Evidence from Germany. *International Tax and Public Finance*. 9. pp. 631–649.

T. Baskaran and L. Feld. 2013. Fiscal Decentralization and Economic Growth in OECD Countries: Is There a Relationship? *Public Finance Review*. 41 (4). pp. 421–445.

T. Besley and R. Burgess. 2002 The Political Economy of Government Responsiveness: Theory and Evidence from India. *Quarterly Journal of Economics*. 117 (4). pp. 1415–1451.

R. M. Bird and F. Vaillancourt. 1998. Fiscal Decentralization in Developing Countries: An Overview. *Fiscal Decentralization in Developing Countries*. 1. pp. 1–48.

A. Blazey and M. Lelong. 2022. Green Budgeting: A Way Forward. *OECD Journal on Budgeting*. 22/2. https://doi.org/10.1787/dc7ac5a7-en.

H. Blöchliger et al. 2007. *Fiscal Equalisation in OECD Countries*. Organisation for Economic Co-operation and Development.

B. Bollinger and S. E. Sexton. 2023. Local Excise Taxes, Sticky Prices, and Spillovers: Evidence from Berkeley's Soda Tax. *Quantitative Marketing and Economics*. 21 (2). pp. 281–331.

Y. Bury and L. Feld. 2023. Fiscal Federalism in Germany. In J. F. Tremblay (ed.) *The Forum of Federations Handbook of Fiscal Federalism*. Cham: Palgrave Macmillan.

H. Cai and D. Treisman. 2006. Did Government Decentralization Cause China's Economic Miracle? *World Politics*. 58 (4). pp. 505–535.

Canada Department of Finance. 2006. *Achieving a National Purpose: Putting Equalization Back on Track*. Ottawa: Canada Department of Finance.

D. H. Chen and C. J. Dahlman. 2005. The Knowledge Economy, the KAM Methodology and World Bank Operations. *Working Paper 37256*. World Bank Institute.

J. Y. S. Cheng. 2018. *The Development of Guangdong: China's Economic Powerhouse.* World Scientific.

H. Chernick. 2003. Fiscal Equalisation Between Swedish Municipalities. *National Tax Journal.* pp. 185–191.

Commonwealth Grants Commission (CGC). 2020. *2020 Review – Horizontal Fiscal Equalization.* CGC.

———. 2022. *Some International Themes in Fiscal Equalisation: An Australian Perspective.* CGC.

B. Dahlby. 2008. The Canadian Federal-Provincial Fiscal Equalization System. https://www.ifo.de/DocDL/dicereport108-forum1.pdf.

S. Dougherty and F. Forman. 2021. *Evaluating Fiscal Equalisation: Finding the Right Balance.* Organisation for Economic Co-operation and Development.

European Commission. 2024. Forging a Sustainable Future Together – Cohesion for a Competitive and Inclusive Europe. *Report of the High-Level Group on the Future of Cohesion Policy.* Brussels-Luxembourg: Publications Office of the European Union.

European Committee of the Regions. 2024. Germany – Fiscal Powers. https://portal.cor.europa.eu/divisionpowers/Pages/Germany-Fiscal-Powers.aspx.

R. Ezcurra and P. Pascual. 2008. The Link Between Fiscal Decentralization and Regional Disparities: Evidence from Several European Union Countries. *Environment and Planning A.* 40 (5). pp. 1185–1201.

C. S. Fan, C. Lin, and D. Treisman. 2009. Political Decentralization and Corruption: Evidence from Around the World. *Journal of Public Economics.* 93 (1–2). pp. 14–34.

T. Farole, A. Rodríguez-Pose, and M. Storper. 2011. Cohesion Policy in the European Union: Growth, Geography, Institutions. *Journal of Common Market Studies.* 49 (5). pp. 1089–1111.

F. Fitrani, B. Hofman, and K. Kaiser. 2005. Unity in Diversity? The Creation of New Local Governments in a Decentralising Indonesia. *Bulletin of Indonesian Economic Studies.* 41 (1). pp. 57–79.

Government of Canada. 2024. Equalization Program. https://www.canada.ca/en/department-finance/programs/federal-transfers/equalization.html.

Government of Kazakhstan. 2024. President Kassym-Jomart Tokayev's State of the Nation Address Just Kazakhstan: Law and Order, Economic Growth, Social Optimism. https://akorda.kz/en/president-kassym-jomart-tokayevs-state-of-the-nation-address-just-kazakhstan-law-and-order-economic-growth-social-optimism-482433.

E. J. Grin et al. 2021. Together It Is Possible to Go Further: Brazilian Health Inter-Municipal Consortium as a Collaborative and Innovative Governance to Fight COVID-19. *International Research Society for Public Management.*

Gujarat Infrastructure Development Board (GIDB). 2024. Public–Private Partnerships. GIDB. https://www.gidb.org/public-private-partnership.

B. Harris. 2017. The Astonishing Rise of Shenzhen, China's Gadget Capital. World Economic Forum. 9 November. https://www.weforum.org/stories/2017/11/inside-shenzhen-china-s-gadget-capital/.

Y. Hegele and N. Behnke. 2017. Horizontal Coordination in Cooperative Federalism: The Purpose of Ministerial Conferences in Germany. *Regional & Federal Studies.* 27 (5). pp. 529–548.

S. Iammarino, A. Rodriguez-Pose, and M. Storper. 2019. Regional Inequality in Europe: Evidence, Theory and Policy Implications. *Journal of Economic Geography.* 19 (2). pp. 273–298.

Indian Institute of Public Affairs (IIPA). 2022. PPPs and Negotiating Strategies. IIPA. https://www.iipa.org.in/cms/public/training_course/32.

Institute for Government. 2018. *Tax and Devolution*. Institute for Government.

Inter-American Development Bank (IDB). 2023. Fortalecimiento de la gestión fiscal subnacional: lecciones y aprendizajes desde el terreno (2010–2020). IDB.

International Monetary Fund (IMF). 2024. *Republic of Kazakhstan: 2023 Article IV Consultation–Press Release; Staff Report; and Statement by the Executive Director for Republic of Kazakhstan*. IMF.

InvestSP. 2024. Investment Incentive Policies. https://www.en.investe.sp.gov.br/why-sao-paulo/incentive-policies/.

M. Ivanyna and A. Shah. 2011. Decentralization and Corruption: New Cross-Country Evidence. *Environment and Planning C: Government and Policy*. 29 (2). pp. 344–362.

H. Jin, Y. Qian, and B. R. Weingast. 2005. Regional Decentralization and Fiscal Incentives: Federalism, Chinese Style. *Journal of Public Economics*. 89 (9–10). pp. 1719–1742.

D. Kazbekova et al. 2024. Mechanisms of Stimulation of Small- and Medium-Sized Entrepreneurship: The Experience of Kazakhstan. *Journal of Risk and Financial Management*. 17 (7). p. 257.

H. Kharas and H. Kohli. 2011. What Is the Middle Income Trap, Why Do Countries Fall into It, and How Can It Be Avoided? *Global Journal of Emerging Market Economies*. 3 (3). pp. 281–289.

H. Kitchen. 2012. Property Tax: A Situation Analysis and Overview. *A Primer on Property Tax – Administration and Policy*. pp. 1–40.

A. P. Kyriacou, L. Muinelo-Gallo, and O. Roca-Sagalés. 2017. Fiscal Decentralization and Regional Disparities: The Importance of Good Governance. *Papers in Regional Science*. 96 (3). pp. 579–598.

C. Lessmann and G. Markwardt. 2016. Aid, Growth, and Devolution: Considering Aid Modality and Different Types of Decentralization. *World Development*. 84. pp. 118–130.

W. L. Lin and T. P. Chen. 2004. China's Widening Economic Disparities and Its "Go West Program." *Journal of Contemporary China*. 13 (41). pp. 663–686.

L. A. Lindau, D. Hidalgo, and D. Facchini. 2010. Bus Rapid Transit in Curitiba, Brazil: A Look at the Outcome After 35 Years of Bus-Oriented Development. *Transportation Research Record*. 2193 (1). pp. 17–27.

K. Lindert et al. 2007. The Nuts and Bolts of Brazil's Bolsa Família Program: Implementing Conditional Cash Transfers in a Decentralized Context. *Social Protection Discussion Paper 709*. World Bank.

J. López-Laborda and J. Onrubia. 2005. Personal Income Tax Decentralization, Inequality, and Social Welfare. *Public Finance Review*. 33 (2). pp. 213–235.

J. Ma. 1997. *Intergovernmental Fiscal Transfer: A Comparison of Nine Countries (Cases of the United States, Canada, the United Kingdom, Australia, Germany, Japan, Korea, India, and Indonesia)*. World Bank.

J. Martínez-Vázquez, S. Lago-Peñas, and A. Sacchi. 2017. The Impact of Fiscal Decentralization: A Survey. *Journal of Economic Surveys*. 31 (4). pp. 1095–1129.

J. Martínez-Vázquez and R. M. McNab. 2003. Fiscal Decentralization and Economic Growth. *World Development*. 31 (9). pp. 1597–1616.

T. Morgan. 2024. Federal, NT Governments Announces 10-year, $4 Billion Remote Housing Agreement. *ABC*. 11 March. https://www.abc.net.au/news/2024-03-12/10-year-nt-remote-housing-agreement-worth-4-billion-announcement/103574262.

A. Nakispekova. 2024. Kazakhstan Sparks Innovation and Empowers Entrepreneurs for Economic Advancement. *Astana Times*. 2 January. https://astanatimes.com/2024/01/kazakhstan-sparks-innovation-and-empowers-entrepreneurs-for-economic-advancement/.

N. A. Nazarbayev. 2012. *Address by the President of the Republic of Kazakhstan: Kazakhstan Strategy 2050.*

P. O'Brien and A. Pike. 2015. The Governance of Local Infrastructure Funding and Financing. *Infrastructure Complexity*. 2. pp. 1–9.

Organisation for Economic Co-operation and Development (OECD). 2017. *Decentralisation and Multi-Level Governance in Kazakhstan*. OECD.

———. 2020a. *OECD Tax Policy Reviews: Kazakhstan 2020*. OECD.

———. 2020b. *Regional Policies to Support Diversification and Productivity Growth in Kazakhstan*. OECD.

———. 2022. *A Practical Guide to Developing and Advancing Tax Capacity Building Programmes*. OECD.

———. 2023a. *The Global Revenue Statistics Database 2023*. OECD.

———. 2023b. *Revenue Statistics 2023: Tax Revenue Buoyancy in OECD Countries*. OECD.

———. 2024a. *Adapting Intergovernmental Fiscal Transfers for the Future: Emerging Trends and Innovative Approaches*. OECD.

———. 2024b. *Diversifying Kazakhstan's Exports: Institutions, Policies, Infrastructures*. OECD.

M. A. Porrúa, F. Baudino, and E. Faba. 2022. 8 Lessons from Estonia's Digital Transformation for Latin America and the Caribbean. *Inter-American Development Bank blog*. 20 December. https://blogs.iadb.org/administracion-publica/en/8-lessons-from-estonias-digital-transformation-for-latin-america-and-the-caribbean/.

R. Prud'homme. 1995. The Dangers of Decentralisation. *The World Bank Research Observer*. pp. 201–220.

Republic of Kazakhstan. 2021. How Nurly Zhol Program Is Changing Kazakhstan: Modern Highways and New Directions. https://primeminister.kz/en/news/reviews/how-nurly-zhol-program-is-changing-kazakhstan-modern-highways-and-new-directions.

A. Rodríguez-Pose. 2018. The Revenge of the Places That Don't Matter (and What to Do About It). *Cambridge journal of Regions, Economy and Society*. 11 (1). pp. 189–209.

———. 2002. The Role of the ILO in Implementing Local Economic Development Strategies in a Globalized World. *Policy Paper. Geneva: International Labour Organization.*

A. Rodríguez-Pose and F. Bartalucci. 2021. *Regional Inequality Study for Kazakhstan*. ADB.

A. Rodríguez-Pose and R. Ezcurra. 2010. Does Decentralisation Matter for Regional Disparities? A Cross-Country Analysis. *Journal of Economic Geography*. 10 (5). pp. 619–644.

A. Rodríguez-Pose and T. D. Ketterer. 2020. Institutional Change and the Development of Lagging Regions in Europe. *Regional Studies*. 54 (7). pp. 974–986.

A. Rodríguez-Pose et al. 2024a. Assessing Regional Inequalities in Kazakhstan Through Well-Being. *Asian Development Review*. 41 (1). pp. 301–333.

A. Rodríguez-Pose et al. 2024b. Overcoming Left-Behindedness. Moving Beyond the Efficiency Versus Equity Debate in Territorial Development. *Regional Science Policy & Practice*. 16 (12). p. 100144.

S. Sakenova. 2024. President Tokayev Approves National Development Plan Until 2029. *Astana Times*. 7 August. https://astanatimes.com/2024/08/president-tokayev-approves-national-development-plan-until-2029/.

SALGA. 2020. Municipal Capabilities. South African Local Government Association. https://www.salga.org.za/Salga%20-%20MCnHR.html.

A. Satubaldina. 2023. Experts Weigh in on Tokayev's Warning of New Economic Abnormality and New Government Tasks. *Astana Times*. 21 April. https://astanatimes.com/2023/04/experts-weigh-in-on-tokayevs-warning-of-new-economic-abnormality-and-new-government-tasks/.

C. F. Sepúlveda and J. Martínez-Vázquez. 2011. The Consequences of Fiscal Decentralization on Poverty and Income Inequality. *Environment and Planning C: Government and Policy*. 29 (2). pp. 321–343.

J. Serra and J. Afonso. 2007. Fiscal Federalism in Brazil: An Overview. *CEPAL Review*. 91. pp. 29–51.

A. Shah. 2006. *A Practitioner's Guide to Intergovernmental Fiscal Transfers*. World Bank.

———. 2007. Fiscal Need Equalization: Is It Worth Doing? Lessons from International Practices. *Working Paper*. World Bank.

———. 2017. *Horizontal Fiscal Equalization in Australia: Peering Inside the Black Box*. Australian Government Productivity Commission.

C. Shen, J. Jin, and H. F. Zou. 2012. Fiscal Decentralization in China: History, Impact, Challenges and Next Steps. *Annals of Economics & Finance*. 13 (1).

R. Shotton and U. Gankhuyag. 2021. Fiscal Transfers in Asia: Pitfalls and Opportunities for Achieving the Sustainable Development Goals. In J. Kim and S. Dougherty (eds). *Local Public Finance and Capacity Building in Asia: Issues and Challenges*. OECD.

D. Silva Rodrigues et al. 2021. Influence of the Municipal Participation Fund and Fiscal Responsibility on the Level of Socioeconomic Development of Brazilian Municipalities. *Revista Contemporânea de Contabilidade*. 18 (49).

M. Sow and M. I. F. Razafimahefa. 2015. *Fiscal Decentralization and the Efficiency of Public Service Delivery*. IMF.

J. Steffensen. 2010. Performance-Based Grant Systems: Concept and International Experience. United Nations Capital Development Fund. http://www.uncdf.org/en/node/2304.

Tasmanian Government. 2024. *Backing Our Tourism Industry*. Tasmania: Tasmanian Government.

T. Ter-Minassian. 2021. Challenges of Subnational Capacity Development. In J. Kim and S. Dougherty (eds). *Local Public Finance and Capacity Building in Asia: Issues and Challenges*. OECD.

Z. Wang and L. Ma. 2014. Fiscal Decentralization in China: A Literature Review. *Annals of Economics & Finance*. 15 (2).

S. Wang and D. Y. Yang. 2021. Policy Experimentation in China: The Political Economy of Policy Learning. *Working Paper w29402*. National Bureau of Economic Research.

A. Wiedenbach. 2021. The Chinese Government as Solar Power Entrepreneur and the Examples of Suntech and Longi Green Energy Technology Company. *China News Brief and Action Alert*. https://www.climatescorecard.org/2021/04/the-chinese-government-as-solar-power-entrepreneur-and-the-examples-of-suntech-and-longi-green-energy-technology-company/.

C. P. Wong. 2000. Central-Local Relations Revisited: The 1994 Tax-Sharing Reform and Public Expenditure Management in China. *China Perspectives*. pp. 52–63.

World Bank. 2021. *Fiscal Decentralization, Local Public Sector Finance And Intergovernmental Fiscal Relations: A Primer*. World Bank.

———. 2022. *Equitable Human Capital Development In Kazakhstan: The State of Human Capital Across the Regions of Kazakhstan*. World Bank.

———. 2024a. World Development Indicators Database. https://databank.worldbank.org/source/world-development-indicators.

———. 2024b. *World Development Report 2024: The Middle-Income Trap*. World Bank.

———. 2024c. *Kazakhstan: Poverty and Equity Assessment*. World Bank.

X. Xiaomin. 2016. Hangzhou's Innovation Efforts Encourage Startup Firms. China Daily. 15 April. http://www.ezhejiang.gov.cn/2016-04/15/c_556764.htm.

www.ingramcontent.com/pod-product-compliance
Lightning Source LLC
Chambersburg PA
CBHW041755220926
51847CB00014B/215
9789292776060